ideals
HARVEST TIME ISSUE

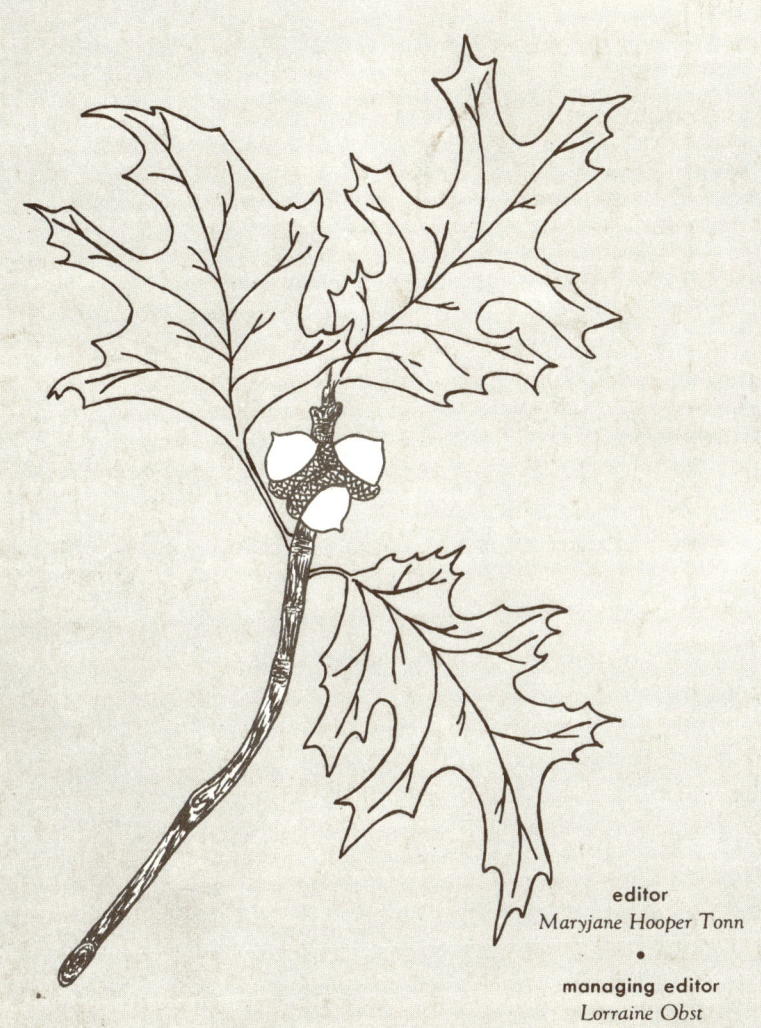

Tall trees
Aflame in gold,
As altars stand,
To celebrate harvest
   and home
And God.

Heidi Knecht

editor
Maryjane Hooper Tonn
•
managing editor
Lorraine Obst
•
assistant managing editor
Ralph Luedtke

IDEALS—Vol. 32, No. 5—September, MCMLXXV. Published bimonthly by IDEALS PUBLISHING CORP., 11315 Watertown Plank Road, Milwaukee, Wis. 53226. Second-class postage paid at Milwaukee, Wisconsin. Copyright © MCMLXXV by IDEALS PUBLISHING CORP. All rights reserved. Title IDEALS registered U.S. Patent Office.

ONE YEAR SUBSCRIPTION—six consecutive issues as published—only $8.50
TWO YEAR SUBSCRIPTION—twelve consecutive issues as published—only $16.00
SINGLE ISSUES—only $2.50

The cover and entire contents of IDEALS are fully protected by copyright and must not be reproduced in any manner whatsoever. Printed and bound in U.S.A.

Indian Summer

It is the Indian summer. The rising sun blazes through the misty air like a conflagration. A yellowish, smoky haze fills the atmosphere, and a filmy mist lies like a silver lining on the sky. The wind is soft and low. It wafts to us the odor of forest leaves, that hang wilted on the dripping branches, or drop into the stream. Their gorgeous tints are gone, as if the autumnal rains had washed them out. Orange, yellow and scarlet, all are changed to one melancholy russet hue. The birds, too, have taken wing, and have left their roofless dwellings. Not the whistle of a robin, not the twitter of an eavesdropping swallow, not the carol of one sweet, familiar voice. All gone. Only the dismal cawing of a crow, as he sits and curses that the harvest is over; or the chit-chat of an idle squirrel, the noisy denizen of a hollow tree, the mendicant friar of a large parish, the absolute monarch of a dozen acorns.

Henry Wadsworth Longfellow

A Day of Reflections

This is a day of reflections,
   Reflections of summer past;
A look to the distant hillsides,
   And down through the valleys vast

Brings panoramas of beauty;
   The trees tinged with rust and gold
Spell autumn in big bold letters;
   How much of splendor they hold!

I see the cornfields stand mutely,
   All shocked and rustling with wind;
I see the pumpkins there sitting
   (And not in the least chagrined!).

Yes, this is a day for reflections;
   I think of the summer past.
But, oh, the beauties of autumn...
   Their grandeur is unsurpassed!

Georgia B. Adams

Dame Summer

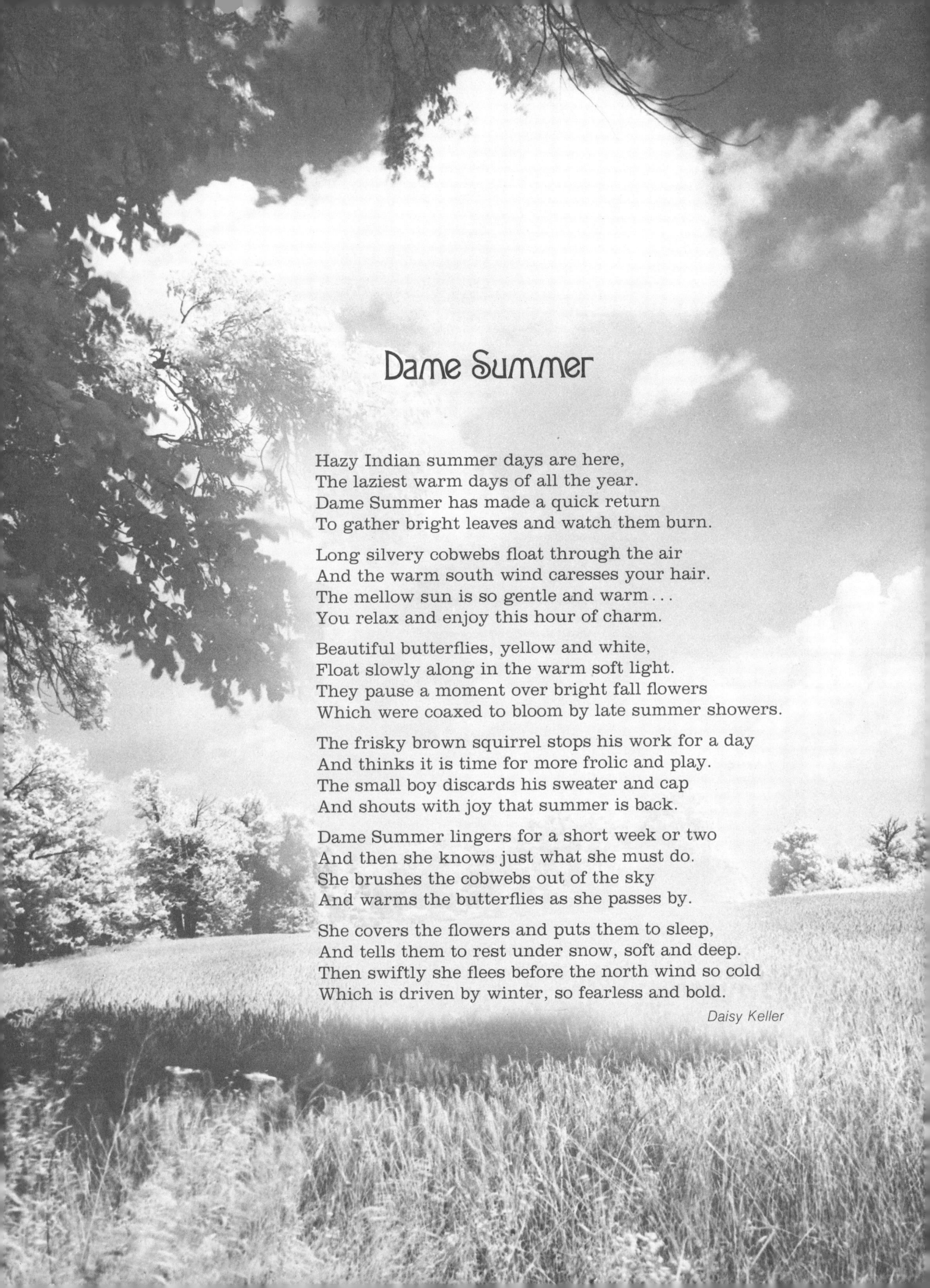

Hazy Indian summer days are here,
The laziest warm days of all the year.
Dame Summer has made a quick return
To gather bright leaves and watch them burn.

Long silvery cobwebs float through the air
And the warm south wind caresses your hair.
The mellow sun is so gentle and warm...
You relax and enjoy this hour of charm.

Beautiful butterflies, yellow and white,
Float slowly along in the warm soft light.
They pause a moment over bright fall flowers
Which were coaxed to bloom by late summer showers.

The frisky brown squirrel stops his work for a day
And thinks it is time for more frolic and play.
The small boy discards his sweater and cap
And shouts with joy that summer is back.

Dame Summer lingers for a short week or two
And then she knows just what she must do.
She brushes the cobwebs out of the sky
And warms the butterflies as she passes by.

She covers the flowers and puts them to sleep,
And tells them to rest under snow, soft and deep.
Then swiftly she flees before the north wind so cold
Which is driven by winter, so fearless and bold.

Daisy Keller

Autumn Trail

The trail is a ribbon of sunlight
That meanders through the trees,
Fringed by the boughs of autumn
And kissed by the falling leaves;
A way unrolled before me
Wending deep into autumn's fold
Where the wondrous world of beauty
Is waiting for me to behold.

The woods are ablaze with color
Along the trail's domain
Where I tremble beneath the glow
Of maples wrapped in fiery flames,
And I cannot quench the flares
Resplendent with yellow light...
The aspens in their glistening robes
That ever glow more bright.

Up and along the gleaming trail,
Over the hillside and down,
I gather the thrill and sweet reward
Of beauties that richly abound,
And I climb with joy the higher ridge
To see the world unveiled...
To glory in the grander view
That waits...but farther up the trail.

Joy Belle Burgess

Photograph opposite
Jack Zehrt

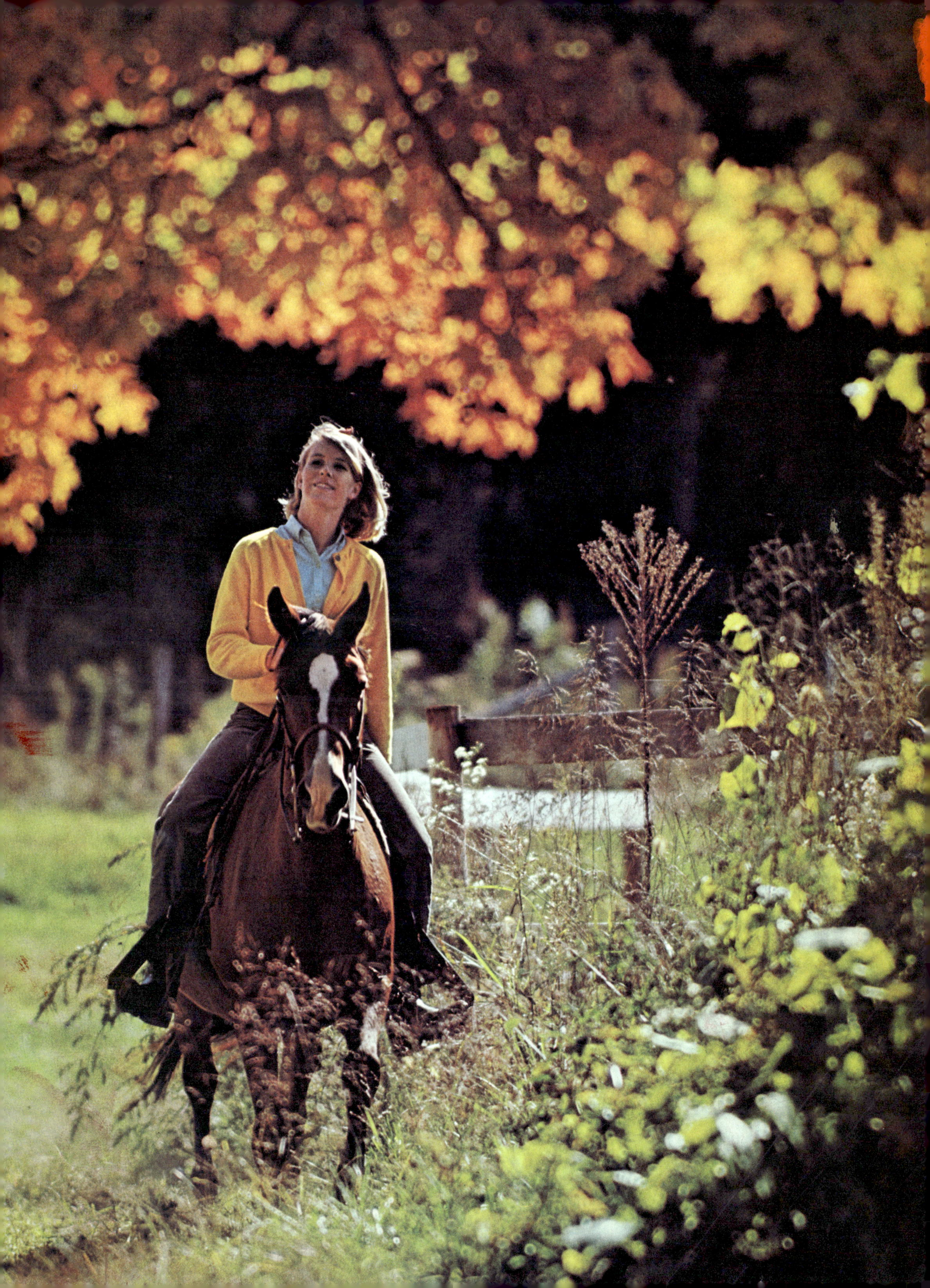

Only October Knows

Only October knows
The full rhythm of the year.

Remembrance of flowering spring
Is in leafage
October has colored,
And taste of summer lingers
In harvested fruit of the autumn.
A shy nip of frost is a fairy-foretelling
Of wintertime's icicle teeth.

Only October's own Indian summer
Sings the year's long rhythm,
Sweet-throbbing and full.

Maude Dickinson

Beautiful October

Samuel Taylor Coleridge, the English poet, once said: *"Why is it that many of us persist in thinking that autumn is a sad season? Nature has merely fallen asleep, and her dreams must be beautiful, if we are to judge by her countenance."* The lovely month of October is in no way a sad time, with the beautiful red and crimson of the leaves and the golden pumpkin in the fields. Someone has said that October is just the happy side of summer and the pleasant side of winter.

Monta Crane

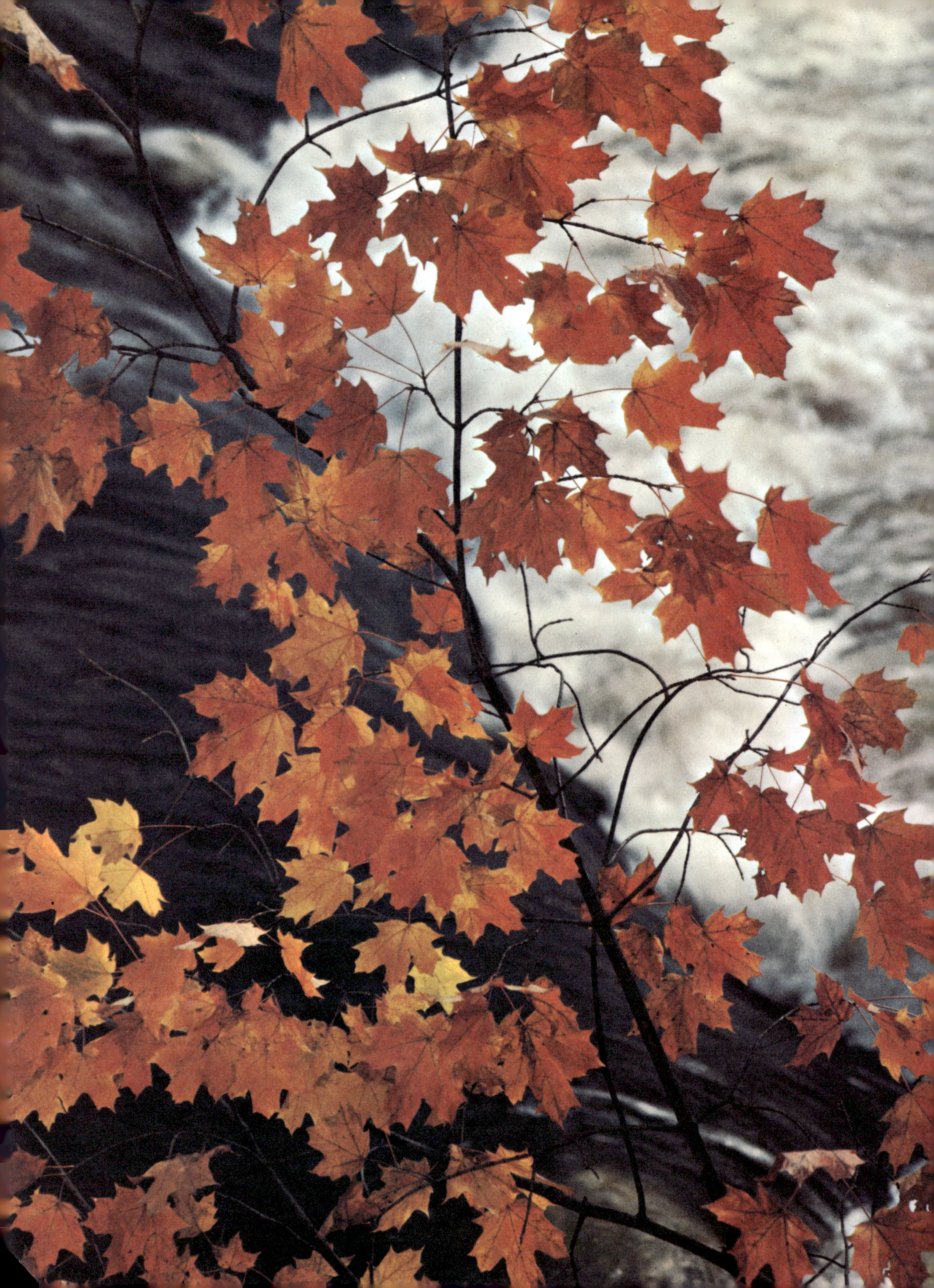

Thanksgiving in Canada

In some respects, Thanksgiving in Canada is similar to the holiday in the United States. It is an autumn celebration which originated with a thanks offering by early New World settlers. It has become a harvest-related festival which is marked by bountiful dinners and large family reunions.

The Canadian Thanksgiving, however, is no mere imitation of the United States celebration, and its roots go back farther than many people realize. It is believed that the first formal Thanksgiving in the New World was celebrated in Canada in 1578—forty-two years before the Pilgrims landed in what was to become Massachusetts.

Sir Martin Frobisher was a British explorer who made several voyages to the New World during the sixteenth century. He was searching primarily for the Northwest Passage, but on one journey he found a sample of ore which he believed to be gold. Upon returning to England, he organized a gold-mining expedition which sailed to Newfoundland in 1578 in an attempt to found a permanent settlement.

It was here that the first American Thanksgiving was reportedly celebrated. Sir John Frobisher, brother of Sir Martin and co-organizer of the expedition, led the service, which offered thanks for the travelers' safe journey to the New World.

The ore which Frobisher had discovered was not really gold, and the settlement did not survive. In fact, no sixteenth-century attempt to establish an American colony turned out to be permanent. It was with this expedition, though, that the idea of celebrating Thanksgiving in the New World originated.

Thanksgiving did not become an annual autumn holiday in Canada until 1879. For many years the celebrations were held on the fourth Thursday in November, the day of the United States holiday. While attempts to change the date in the United States have never succeeded, the Canadian celebration went through a number of changes before a permanent date was established.

First, the day on which the holiday was celebrated was changed from a Thursday to a Monday. Canadian officials felt that it was necessary to provide more traveling time before this day of reunions, so Thanksgiving became the last day of a three-day weekend. After the end of World War I, the date was changed again. At that time the holiday was moved to Monday of the week of November 11th and became associated with Armistice Day festivities.

The final change came in 1931, when Canadians decided that a harvest festival in a land of early winters should not be held so late in the season. In that year they began celebrating Thanksgiving on the second Monday in October. This date apparently satisfies most Canadians, because it has remained unchanged for forty-four years.

Photograph opposite
Rapids in Gatineau Hills
Limbour, Quebec, Canada
Photo—Malak

Tawny
  autumn season
    warmed by the
      sun's red disc,
cradled by the
  burning blue sky
    of noon.

Maude Dickinson

Harvest and Homecoming

Merry Autumn Days

'Tis pleasant on a fine spring morn
To see the buds expand;
'Tis pleasant in the summertime
To see the fruitful land;

'Tis pleasant on a winter's night
To sit around the blaze,
But what are joys like these, my boys,
To merry autumn days!

We hail the merry autumn days,
When leaves are turning red;
Because they're far more beautiful
Than anyone has said,

We hail the merry harvesttime,
The gayest of the year;
The time of rich and bounteous crops,
Rejoicing and good cheer.

Charles Dickens

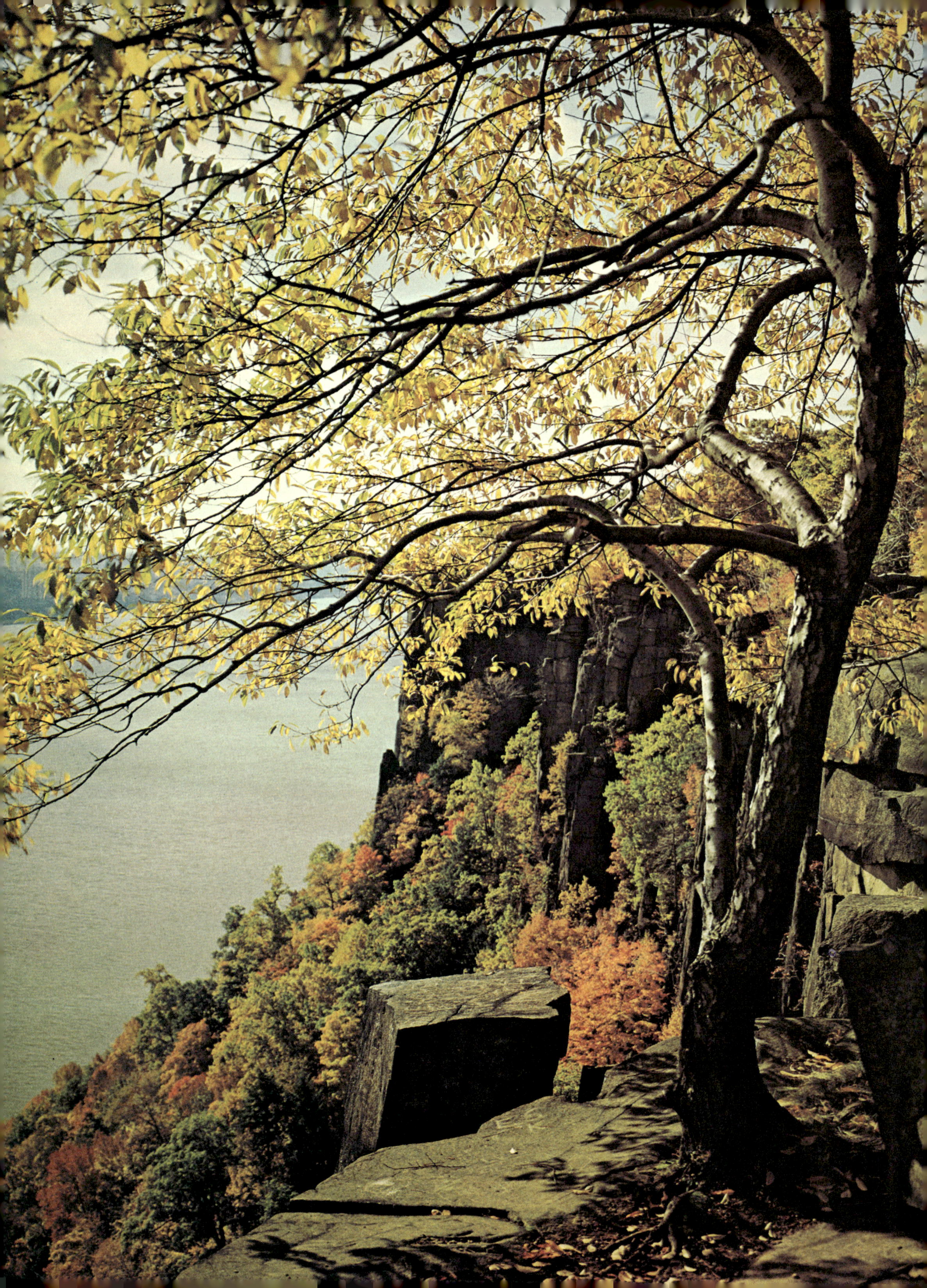

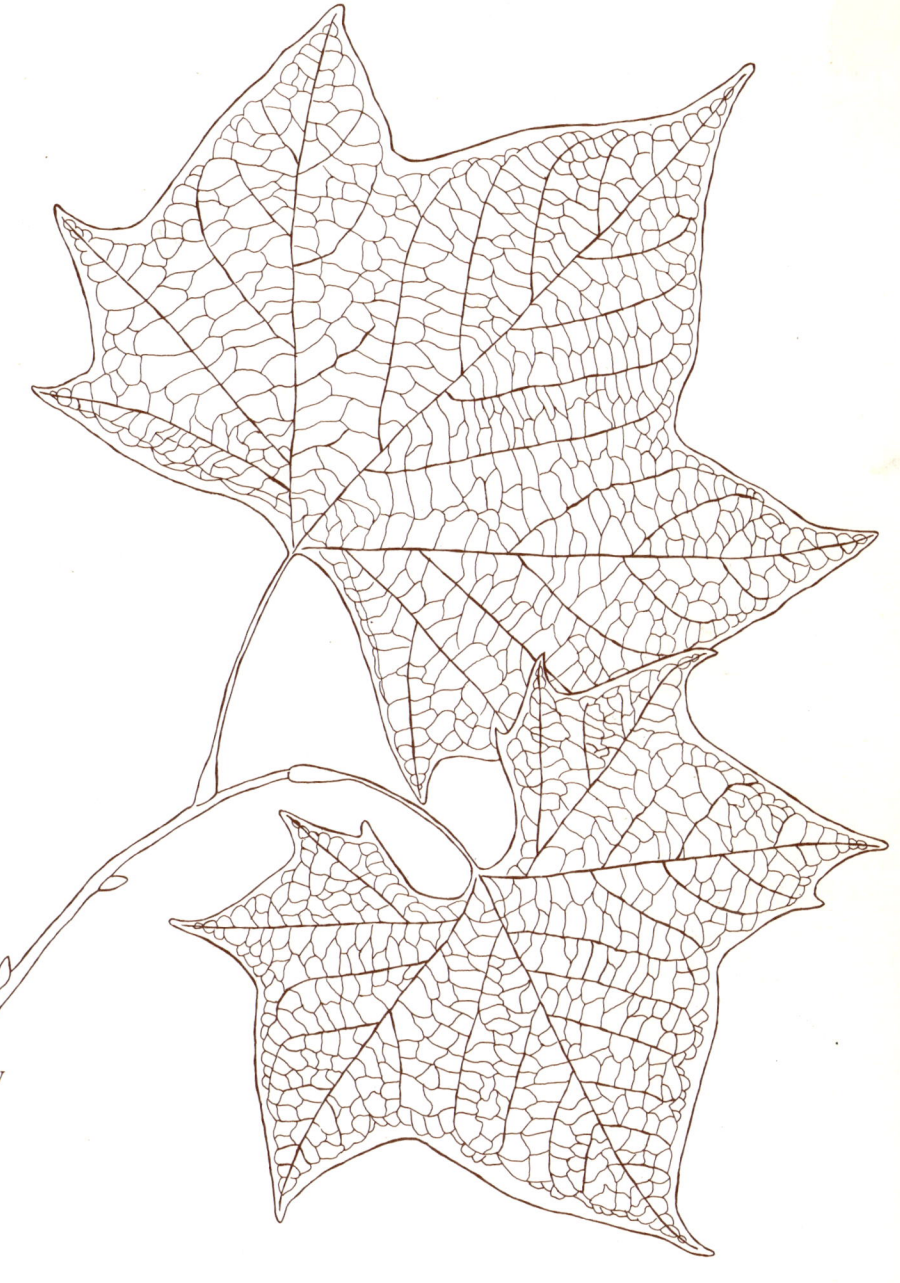

Phantom Fires

Sycamores, warm-golden now,
are tinder for the sun
that lights in them a phantom fire
where tree-filled canyons run.

Boulders, flecked with maple glow
along the dry stream bed
are simmering in cauldrons
of fallen leaves, fire-red.

Autumn air ignites the heart
with crisp-leaved dreams returning
where flame and glory recklessly
pile memories for burning!

Lorraine Babbitt

Photograph opposite
Palisades of New Jersey
Hudson River
Photo—Gene Ahrens

To Walk With Autumn

There may be other times as good as late October to go out afoot and see the world, but there certainly isn't a better one. To walk with the scuffle of new-fallen leaves, to feel the mild sun and see the Autumn sky, to have the company of busy squirrels in the woods and restless ducks on the river, is to sense the season at first hand. To look at the hills in their true dimensions and see to the end of the valleys whence the frost came creeping down last night is to know a world that has achieved the annual miracle.

Walk the country roads and the open fields now and you are a witness to great events accomplished. The sugar maples stand in deep pools of their own leaf gold. The goldenrod is graceful and gray with ripeness. The milkweed offers a richness of silk and seed to every breeze. The white oaks, still brown and crimson with persistent leaves, have planted tomorrow's groves in their own shade. The jack-in-the-pulpit has summarized its own sermon on immortality in a cluster of lacquer-red berries.

Yesterday is all around you, last Spring's growth and last Summer's maturity and last month's ripeness. But tomorrow is there too, the sprout, the leaf, the blossom, waiting only for another Spring. The ripeness is but a part of the continuity, achievement rather than completion. We think of it as the evening of the year; but after the dusk comes starlight, and dawn, and another day. To walk with Autumn is to be in the presence of forever.

Hal Borland

Reprinted by permission of Collins-Knowlton-Wing. From SUNDIAL OF THE SEASONS by Hal Borland. Copyright © 1961 by Hal Borland.

The attractive hardwood frame, size 8½ x 11", with its fruitwood finish, as shown on the opposite page, is perfectly suitable for Ideals pictures. Order it through the Special Selections listed on the order blank. Picture not included.

Painting opposite
WOODCOCKS
by Harry Moeller

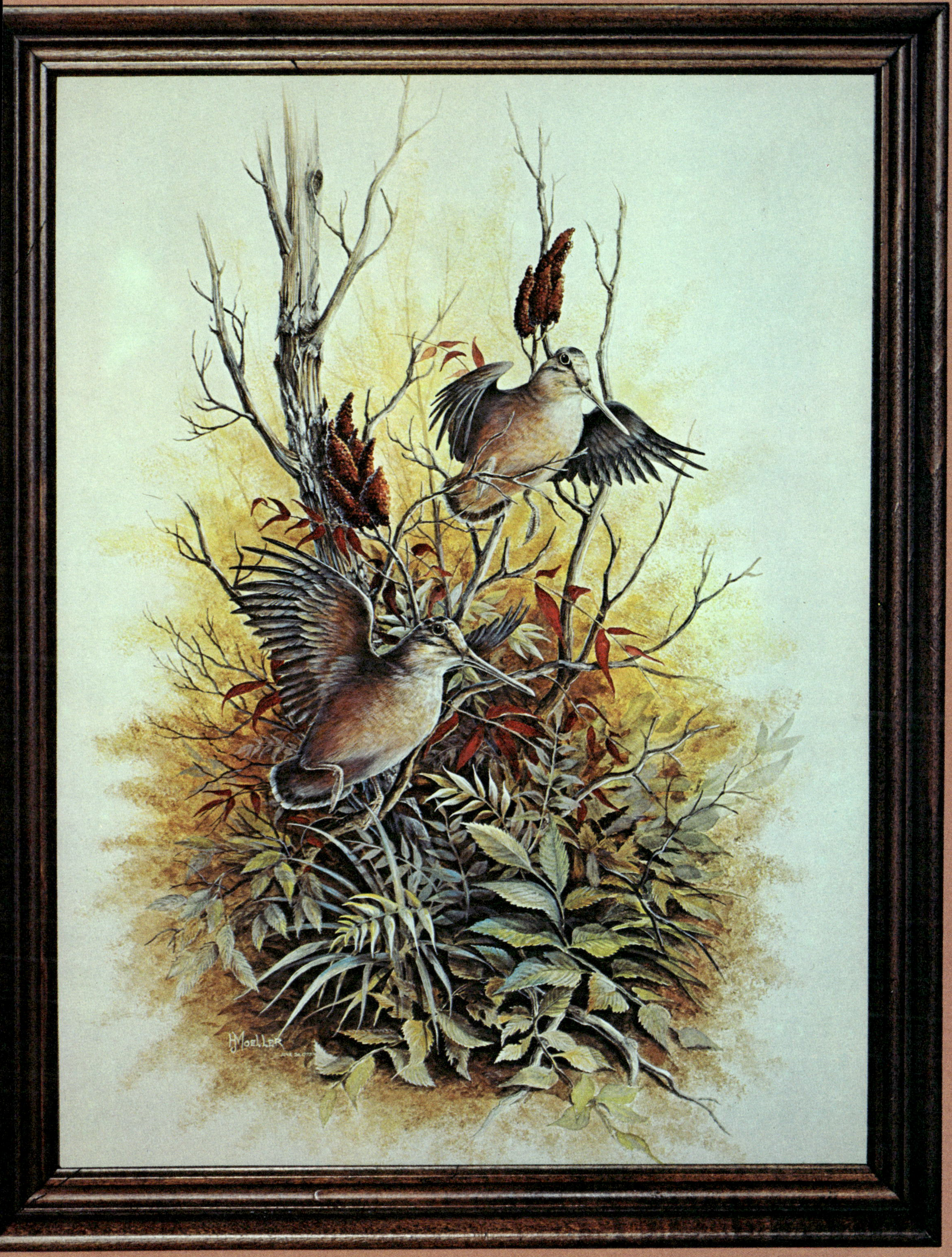
H.MOELLER

A Vagabond Song

There is something in the autumn
   that is native to my blood...
Touch of manner, hint of mood;
And my heart is like a rhyme,
With the yellow and the purple
   and the crimson keeping time.

The scarlet of the maples
   can shake me like a cry
Of bugles going by;
And my lonely spirit thrills
To see the frosty asters
   like a smoke upon the hills.

There is something in October
   sets the gypsy blood astir;
We must rise and follow her
When from every hill of flame
She calls and calls
   each vagabond by name.

Bliss Carman

When the Great Blue Heron Flies

The Great Blue Heron is flying
And his strong wings tug at my heart;
For again he tells me it's autumn,
And again he says we must part.

The ponds still reflect his shadow
Till the shadow is lost to the sky;
And so it is soon with our summer,
For the heron bids summer good-bye.

Good-bye to the end of the summer;
Good-bye to my friend on the wing.
My eyes shall strain for your coming
When again, when again it is spring.

Minnie Klemme

Tunnel of Gold

Each autumn finds a certain country road
Where slender aspens arching on each side
Have captured sunshine till it overflowed
The leaves that wall and arch a golden tide.

Earth's wealth in purest concentrate is there;
To the grasses' edge this gleaming gold is poured—
A long, hushed corridor of filtered prayer.

Olive C. Leary

Now The Deer Come Back

Now the deer come back with the season turning yellow,
Now the days run short and the grass is thin,
Now that the west holds haze and the sun is mellow:
Here in the field are tracks where the deer have been.
They must have stepped on frost this early morning,
Making their way to the rocky haw-lined creek,
Stopping to sniff the air and lightly scorning
Our silent smokeless house on the hill's tan cheek.
This is the place they crossed, and here they halted,
Leaving sharp marks in the mud along the bank,
This is the way they took, this fence they vaulted
And here the footprints end where the shrub grows rank;
And to think we slept so near, yet so unknowing
This beauty, and the silence of its going!

A. L. Fisher

Covered Bridges

Does anyone build covered bridges now?
They used to mark the country here and there,
Not leaping streams, wide open to the air,
With gallant masonry arched like a brow
Above the water's eye. You hushed, somehow,
Your chatter as the horse-hoofs plodded in,
Thumping the boards, all shadowy but for thin
Bright rays the loosened shingles might allow.

A child could lean out from the carriage seat
And see through ill-set floors the river's trend,
The shaken dust; knee-deep, a docile cow,
Or, far ahead, a picture framed and neat;
The sunny outer world at shadow's end...
Does anyone build covered bridges now?

Jennie Pendleton Hall

WHITE MOUNTAIN NATIONAL FOREST
BRIDGE CONSTRUCTED BY
TOWN OF ALBANY
1858
LOAD
LIMIT

from the editor's scrapbook

Heap high the farmer's winter hoard!
Heap high the golden corn!
No richer gift has Autumn poured
From out her lavish horn.

John Greenleaf Whittier

Children think not of what is past, nor what is to come, but enjoy the present time, which few of us do.

La Bruyere

Gratitude is the memory of the heart.

Massieu

Let us be thankful that there still is sunshine, that we still can glimpse the blue of the sky and in our onward way continue to look up. Let us be thankful for friends with kindly smile and cheerful words. This is a time for grateful thanksgiving.

Author Unknown

Prepare today for tomorrow and forget about yesterday.

Martin Vanbee

What is more cheerful, now, in the fall of the year, than an open wood-fire? Do you hear those little chirps and twitters coming out of that piece of applewood? Those are the ghosts of the robins and bluebirds that sang upon the bough when it was in bloom last spring.

Thomas Bailey Aldrich

God grant me the serenity to accept the things I cannot change . . . courage to change the things I can . . . and wisdom to know the difference.

Reinhold Niebuhr

Autumn ... season of mists and mellow fruitfulness.
John Keats

The door of autumn,
Gold on the one side,
Silver on the other—
Let us pass through softly.
Irene Stanley

The best and noblest lives are those which are set toward high ideals.
Almeron

The beauty of the house is order.
The blessing of the house is contentment.
The glory of the house is hospitality.
The crown of the house is godliness.
Author Unknown

How bravely Autumn paints upon the sky
The gorgeous flame of summer which is fled!
Thomas Hood

There is a time for some things,
And a time for all things;
A time for great things,
And a time for small things.
Cervantes

Autumn abounds in things to delight the sense and the spirit. Trees flaunt a lavishness of color. Fruit ripens and mellows for the eating. The harvest of the year's endeavors has come. And the coolness of the air points to hearthside and holiday and the gathering of friends. It is time to enjoy and to share the abundance that is ours.
Esther York Burkholder

If we can't be thankful for what we receive, we should be thankful for what we escape.
Arnold H. Glascow

The day is done, and the darkness
Falls from the wings of night
As a feather is wafted downward
From an eagle in his flight.
Henry Wadsworth Longfellow

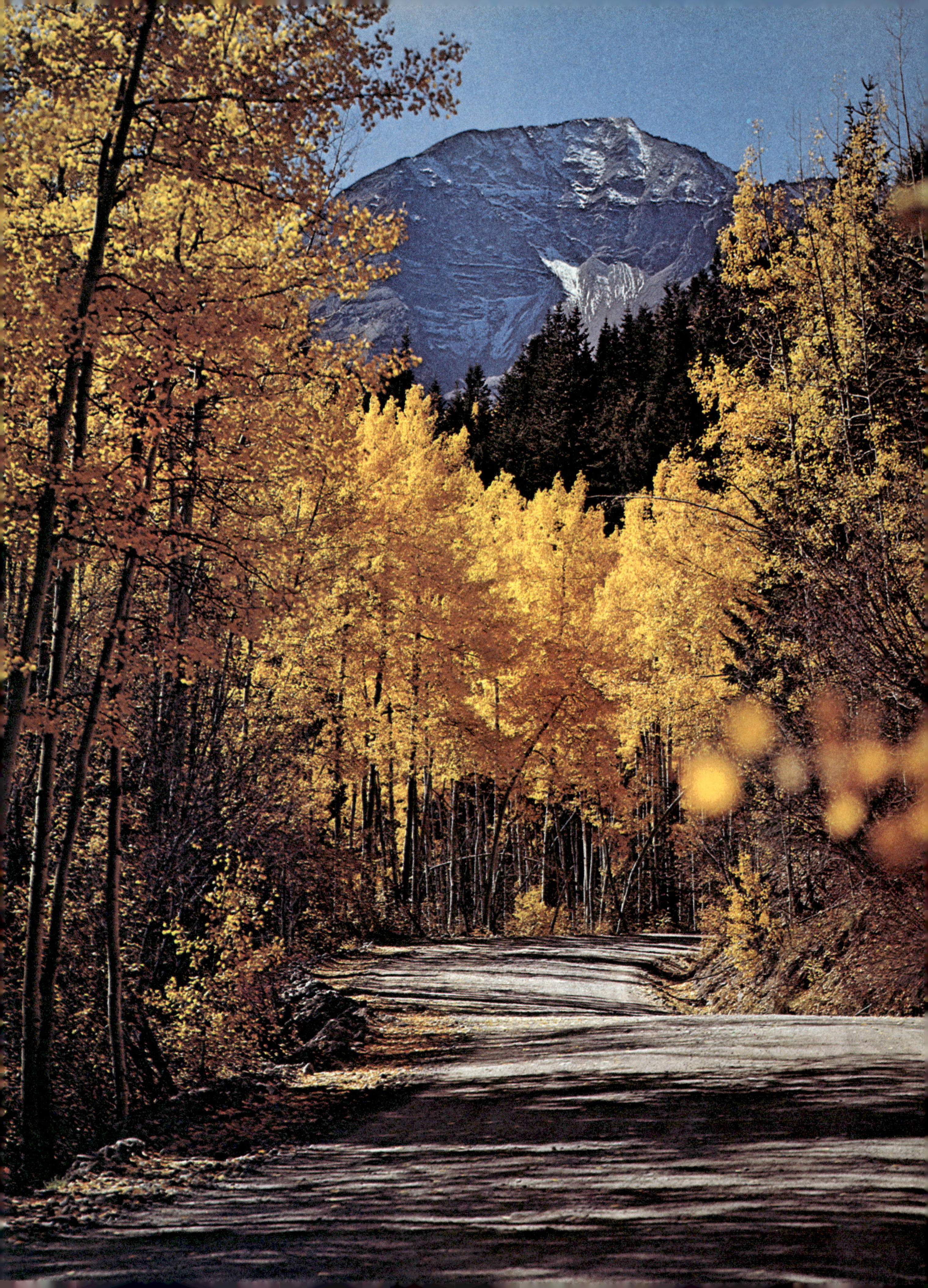

Crisp October Hours

When summer loses its balance and tips with suddenness into the fall of the year, a new era of frost and color unfolds, like a carpet of many hues, over the valleys and the hills. The beauty of the autumn-colored land fans into a glowing appreciation any spark of discontent that a man may harbor in his dreams. The change keeps pace with the passing hours. The wind speaks of it more sharply from day to day, brushing a path for the silvered environment of frosted leaves and grass. There is a vigor in the air; the crisp loud snap of the autumn atmosphere is all around in field and pasture and wood, along a stream.

As if the changing year did not come swiftly enough, rains sweep over the hills and hurry the change along, spreading the flow of color and of frost, keeping in tune with the swiftness of the current of the stream. The liquid fingers of water touch upon the bright October leaves. The hues are even deeper in the golden sun that follows. A countryman is more aware now, after a rain, of the splashing tints of reds and browns and yellows that so brilliantly assume their role over the once-soft green of a summer hill. Unseen pencils and brushes color the land in gowns that soften even the shadows of the night.

One likes to think of the change itself as something like the dawn that pushes its way out of the night. There are the deep dark hours. The next thing, the hour of the dawn has come. So it is with summer, putting aside its green hills and woodlands for a rich autumnal gown. A whole new world seems to have moved in, almost overnight.

Lansing Christman

Photograph opposite Camp Bird Mine Rd. Canyon Creek-San Juan Range, CO. Photo – Freelance Photographer's Guild/ David Muench

The heritage of the past is the seed that brings forth the harvest of the future.

Harvesttime Again

It seems like only yesterday
That we readied the rich black soil
And planted each tiny seedling,
Beginning the springtime toil.

The refreshing little silver drops
Of gentle springtime rain
Watered the thirsty tender shoots
Till the sun came out again.

All of summer they swiftly grew
Reaching higher up each day,
While lovingly we tended them
In a careful tender way.

Now already the harvest
Is ripe and ready to reap,
We'll carefully tuck it safely away
To use when winter is cold and deep.

Ruth H. Underhill

God's Harvest

The time has come to harvest all
The fields of golden grain,
God's bounty overflowing
From every fertile plain.

The haystacks now are ready;
In rows the bundles stand,
Awaiting farmers' wagons.
God bless this fruitful land!

And barn doors that are open
Are gently swinging wide
To welcome all the harvest
That God helped place inside.

Hilda Lorber

Raking Leaves

After the beauty of autumn time
When the leaves have all turned brown,
The trees are stripped of their gaiety
And their wardrobe's fallen down,
There comes an invitation
Which everyone receives,
An inward solicitation
To get busy raking leaves.

Leaf-raking time is sure to come,
So folks don't beat retreat,
But like brave soldiers arm themselves,
And up and down each street
A clean-up squad in every yard,
Each dressed with rolled-up sleeves,
Moves rake and broom in rhythmic time,
While raking up the leaves.

The blaze and smoke of burning leaves
In an evening tableau
Presents some scenes quite picturesque
Concluding autumn's show.
And sometimes a thought in after years
Some loneliness relieves,
When memory flashes to the mind
A scene of raking leaves.

Ottis Shirk

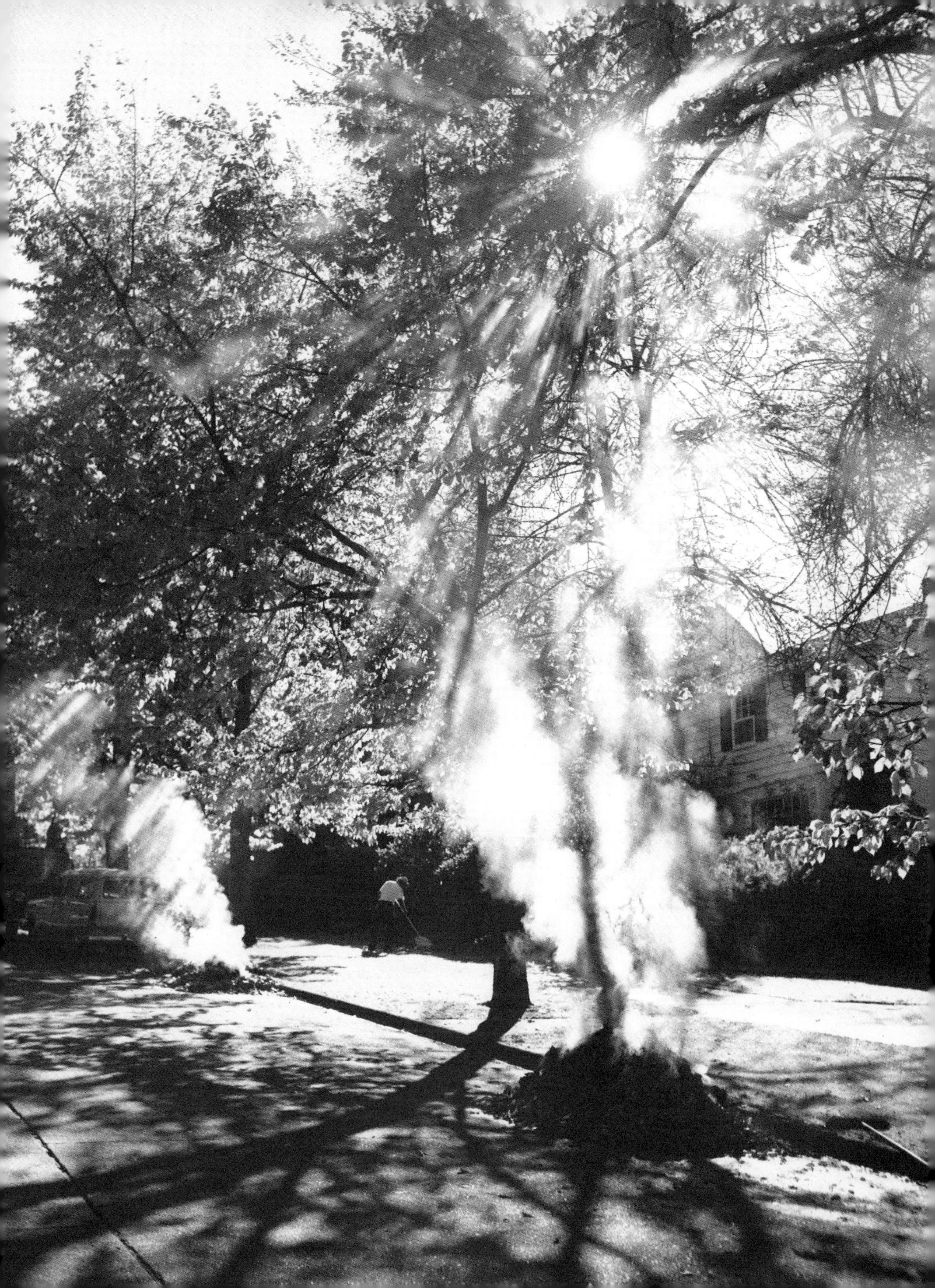

REMEMBER THE MAINE
BREAD
CHEW
George Washington
GREATEST
AMERICAN
CUT
PLUG
CUT PLUG
UNION LEADER
CUT
PLUG
SMOKE AND CHEW
OLD GLORY

TOLEWARE... an American Heirloom

Antique tole has again become popular with collectors. This lacquered tinware, beautifully decorated with painted designs, was fashioned by colonial tinsmiths.

The process of lacquering or "japanning" tin originated in the Orient. In the 18th Century it was brought to America by way of England. In Pontypool, England, tinsmiths developed a varnish which spread to an even coat and could withstand high temperatures. The varnish was hardened in an oven after each coat was applied. Using several coats gave the tinware a shiny, semi-transparent surface.

Tinware became one of England's important exports, and to avoid competition, colonial smiths were forbidden to make or import their own tin plate (the thin sheets of tin-coated iron from which tinware is made). But as tinware became more popular, there was no stopping its production in the colonies.

The techniques used to decorate became more intricate and innovative as demand for tinware increased. One famous practitioner of the art was Paul Revere, who developed a technique of punching holes in the edges of trays to make a lacy pattern. Lace-edged trays came to be called "Paul Revere" trays.

Besides lace edging, there were several other methods of decorating tinware. Designs could be punched into the tin on the reverse side for an embossed effect, or the tin could be engraved. But the most popular decorated tinware was tole—which was lacquered and painted with bright designs.

The most common background color was black, but green, red, yellow and tortoiseshell were also used. Upon this field, the design was stenciled or sketched, then filled in with bright colors and highlights. Typical designs were pastoral scenes and arrangements of fruit or flowers.

Tole was not only decorative. The colonial housewife appreciated tin housewares for their light weight, especially compared to cast iron. And tin, unlike pewter, needed no polishing. The painting of tin gave added protection, since it helped prevent the iron from rusting underneath the tin coat.

So any piece of tinware in the colonial home was likely to be painted and decorated—tea caddies, coffeepots, teapots, boxes, flower holders. The most popular tole items, however, were the trays. These came in all shapes and sizes and were given names according to their uses. There were apple trays, cracker trays, bread trays, tea trays.

In town, tinware could be purchased from the tinsmith. He made the articles and usually decorated them as well, although sometimes a professional artist was called in for the painting. Later, tole painting became a popular lady's home craft.

In rural areas, the source of tinware and tole was the tin peddler, who went from village to village on foot, on horseback, or in a cart. Villagers looked forward to his visits, for besides selling and trading for tinware, the peddler was an important source of news and gossip. Many peddlers were colorful

Toleware courtesy of Mrs. James McCray

Photograph opposite Gerald Koser

characters, and some came to violent ends. According to tradition, Spook Hollow and No Head Hill, New York, were so named because the ghosts of peddlers who were murdered there haunt the scene of the crime.

Tin peddler and smith maintained a close relationship. Sometimes the smith would hire a peddler when the town in which the smith operated had all the tinware it could use. Even if the peddler was independent, he depended on the tinsmith for his merchandise.

The demand for tinware decreased with the coming of the industrial revolution. Soon department stores replaced the tin peddler, and mass-produced housewares usurped the tinsmith's art. The craft itself no longer exists. Those who once created finely crafted, beautifully decorated tinware are today called sheet metal workers.

The techniques of tole painting live on, however, since the craft has been taken up by the hobbyist. Creating modern toleware takes time and patience. The methods are similar to those used in colonial days, although modern materials are easier to work with. But home tole painters say the craft is worthwhile since, in many ways, the finished products are as attractive as antique tole. And they may be heirlooms of the future.

Meaning of Autumn

Bertha R. Hudelson

Autumn is the haunting call
    Of wild geese in the sky,
The purple haze of smoke-filled air,
    A crisp wind passing by.

Autumn is the good-bye note
    Of songbirds southward bound,
The slowing chant of crickets and
    A gold leaf-covered ground.

Autumn is the wizardry
    Of frost with chilling hand,
A deep dust road, grass-hidden paths
    And browning pasture land.

Autumn is the sleeping time
    Of summer's lovely things
Beneath warm blankets pieced of leaves
    And edged with snowflake wings.

THANKSGIVING IN NEW ENGLAND by Missouri Jenkins

Three Lions, Inc.

A Harvest Eve

Hay wagons, heavy-loaded, creak to rest
With stubborn jolts beneath the old loft door;
Tired, dusty men work on with patient zest,
Adding the gracious yield to winter's store.
A flying pigeon makes an easy arc
And sweeps again beneath the shady eaves.
The air is like a summons to embark,
Wild with the fragrance that the new hay leaves.

The stubble field where neatly raked windrows
Lie drying in warm autumnal sun
Suggests a peace profound in its repose,
A call to rest when laboring is done.
A dim nostalgia pervades the air,
And only glowing beauty lingers there.

Webb Dycus

Growing Up

Was it yesterday I laced his shoes,
Wiped his nose and bemoaned each bruise,

Fastened the buttons he couldn't reach
And built sand castles on the beach?

Taught him to count on his ten pink toes,
Listened with care to his little-boy woes,

Plied him with spinach as part of a game,
Guided his hand as he printed his name,

Spanked his bottom and dried his tears,
Scolded and cuddled and calmed his fears,

Tried to explain why the stars twinkled?
(No wonder my brow is perpetually wrinkled!)

Was that yesterday? Why, how time flies!
Today he's a scholar and worldly-wise;

He's not much amused at the jokes we make
And scorns Santa Claus as a silly old fake,

Scoffs at the once-loved Easter rabbit
And terms good-night kisses a babyish habit;

For now he's grown up and so utterly cool...
Today, you see, he started to school.

Betty Heisser

The Old Recitation Bench

'Twas just an old recitation bench,
Barren of paint and defaced,
And it sat outside the little white school,
A "toss-out" of by-gone days.
For the dear little one-room schoolhouse
And all the contents therein
Were ruled "out-of-date" and auctioned off,
But the bench didn't bring a thing!

The names carved upon the weathered wood
Struck a note of memory,
And the wads of gum beneath the seat
Brought a tinge of childish glee.
The lower half of the seat was rough;
The upper half was smooth,
As from the head to tail of the class
The scholars usually moved!

True, the auctioneer asked the bidding crowd
To give an offer fair,
But since no one saw any worth in it,
'Twas unsold and discarded there.
And then in the glow of the after years,
While strolling the old school grounds,
That little old recitation bench
Beneath much debris I found.

'Twas just an old recitation bench,
Barren of paint and defaced,
But to me it was a treasure chest
Of memories of old school days.
And each year as graduation day
Highlights all other events,
'Tis sad to think that progress razed
The old recitation bench.

For a moment only humorous thoughts
Were sketched in my memory;
But then I seemed to faintly recall
How shaky our knees would be
When we'd leave our desks and march up front
As the teacher called our grade,
To sit on the old recitation bench
And recite the progress we made.

Loise Pinkerton Fritz

Overleaf Photograph
Jack Zehrt

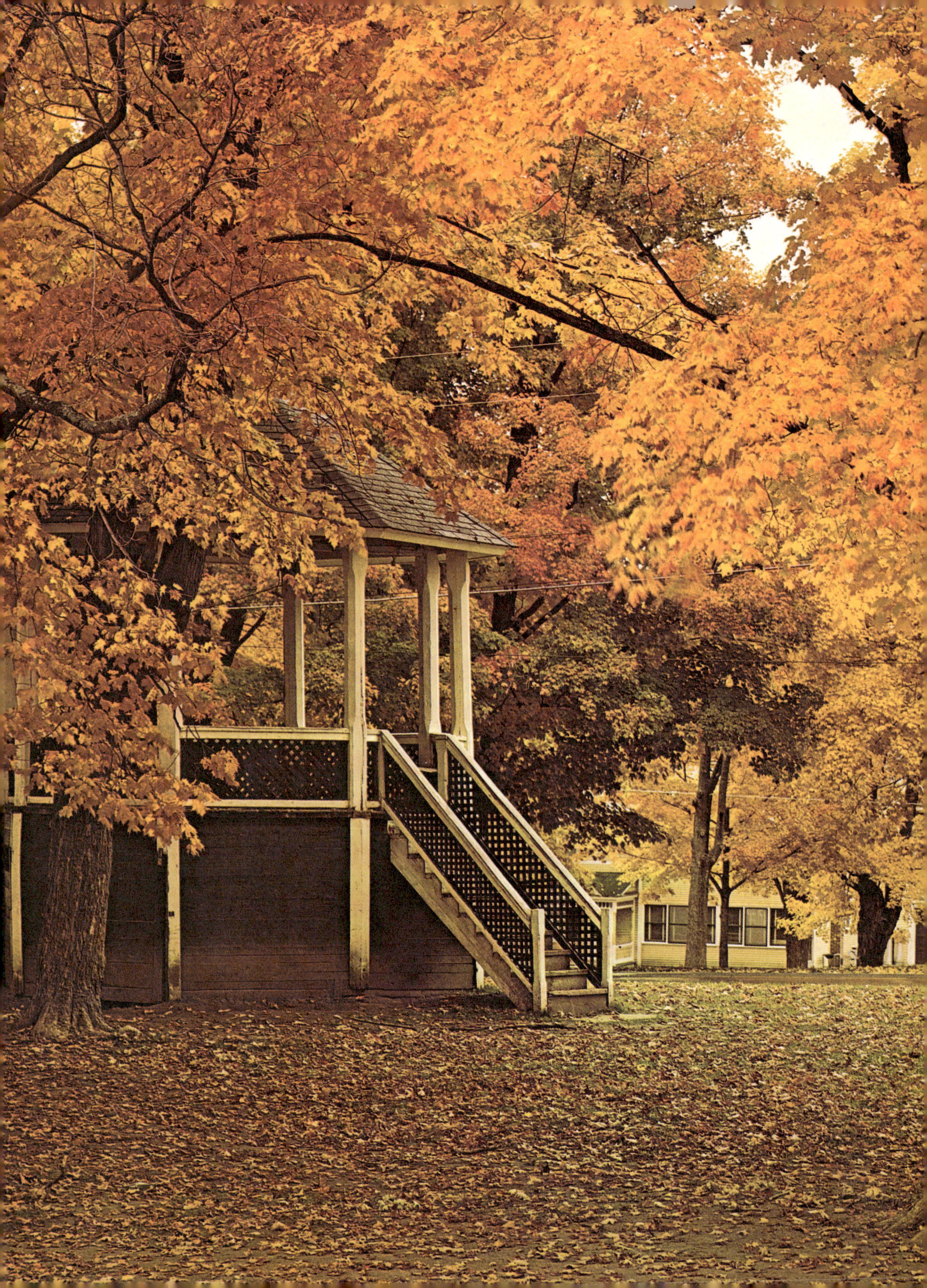

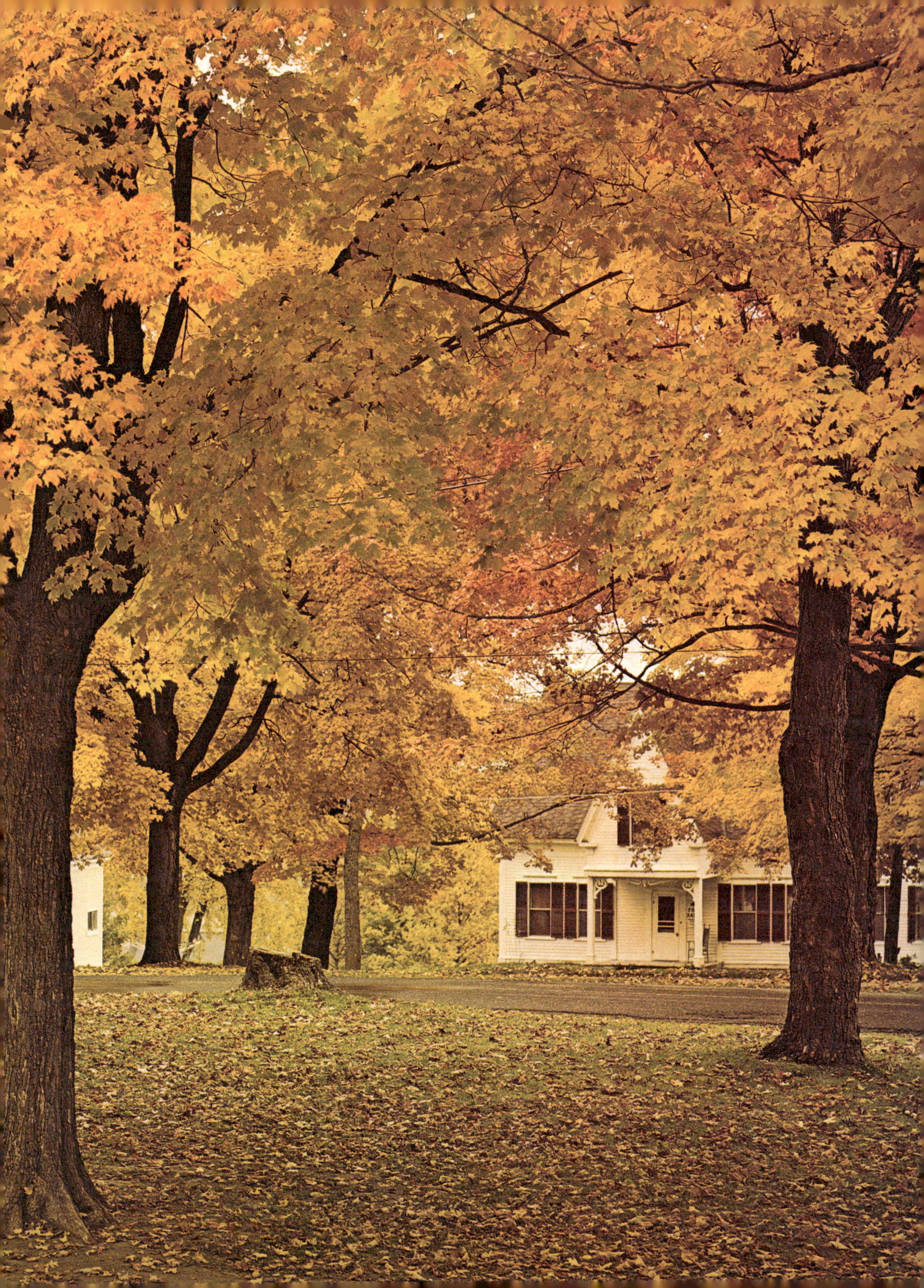

Letter from Home

October is the drama of New England, the time of fulfillment after the hot summer and before the snow drifts deep in the valleys. The air smells of apples and wild grapes and woodsmoke. The trees in our valley blaze with garnet and gold and cinnamon-browns and the deep wine color of the oaks.

Days are crisp and nights meant for an applewood fire on the hearth, a bowl of shiny apples, and plenty of freshly popped corn dredged with butter and salt. At Stillmeadow the two small girls have moved into their fuzzy pajamas with feet (which are so hard to keep clean!). They have their bedtime snack by the fire. Kittens and dogs like to curl up and doze close to the hearth, and the rest of us just fit in around the edges.

Mankind's feeling for the open fire is basic, for in prehistoric times it was the discovery of fire that began man's climb from the jungles. Did lightning start his first one? Or was he rubbing stones together and a spark caught in some dead grass? Fire meant heat and protection from the great beasts, and meat that was cooked. And later some genius discovered that throwing grains and water in a pit of heated stones made a kind of mash that was edible. The charcoal grills as well as the Cape Cod clambake are the present-day version!

In our village we come together at the market, our social center, to discuss when the killing frost will arrive. Everyone is gathering the last garden crops—squash and beets and cabbages and late corn. Rows of jelly glasses glow on the pantry shelves. My favorite is elderberry, with its wine-dark color and tangy flavor—so good with roast lamb or pork.

The commercial jellies and relishes and preserves are delicious and infinite in variety. So all we need to do is "put up a little of this and that," as we say, which makes us feel we are using nature's bounty. In our valley most women have a specialty, and at Christmastime gay jars and bottles are exchanged.

On Cape Cod now the cranberry harvest begins—still gathered in the long-tined scoops that are made of hard maple. The cranberry pickers go through the bogs on hands and knees, combing the berries out with the scoops. The Indians introduced the cranberries to the Pilgrims, but they were small bitter fruits and not the plump spicy jewels of today. Incidentally, one of the best relishes is cranberry relish.

Also on Cape Cod the scallop season begins, and this is a most delicate and savory gift of the sea. Scallops should be broiled very briefly with a bit of lemon juice and melted butter and dashes of paprika and salt.

When the geese go over, the long wedge of their flight arrows the sky with mystery. Do they realize how long the flight will be? How do they decide exactly when to start? Their cry is a lonely sound but breathtaking to hear. Perhaps one reason it is so moving is that it is a farewell to summer. I wish them well as I hear them go over, with a safe coming-back when it is time for them to return.

The next thing we know, the chickadees will be tip-tilting around and chatting away. It is time to clean the bird feeders and get the birdseed in and the cracked corn for the grouse and pheasants. Last winter my son-in-law put out a salt lick, and it was enjoyed; although we never saw the deer, we did see tracks that these visitors had left in the snow.

At the moment there are berries and seeds and a few bugs and spiders, and plenty of nuts for the squirrels. There is time to walk to the pond and see the Hunter's Moon rise and hear the small owl in the apple orchard talking to the night. And time to dream of a world at peace, when the beauty of such a night might fill all hearts.

Daylight saving is over at the end of the month, but as I struggle with the clocks I realize man cannot control time. The sun rises when it is ready to rise and sets when it reaches the time to set. The moon keeps its appointed rounds no matter what our clocks say. I find it reassuring that we cannot yet regulate nature. Nature has a steadiness no nation has yet achieved. And as the seasons come and go, we know it is still a good earth we live on. May we never destroy its wonder.

Gladys Taber

Copyright © 1969 by Family Circle Inc.

Garden Harvest

What pageantry of color
And what beauty so sublime
Have found their way right to my door
This lovely harvesttime!

Tomatoes huge and luscious red
Are ripe to slice and eat,
And golden pumpkins for a pie
Will be a special treat.

The onion garlands hang in wait
Beside the peppers green
While carrots, beans, and ruby beets
Add their hues to the scene.

In baskets waiting at my door
They are a grand display
Of wondrous harvest that will be
A boon on wintry days.

Craig E. Sathoff

Photograph opposite
Fred Sieb

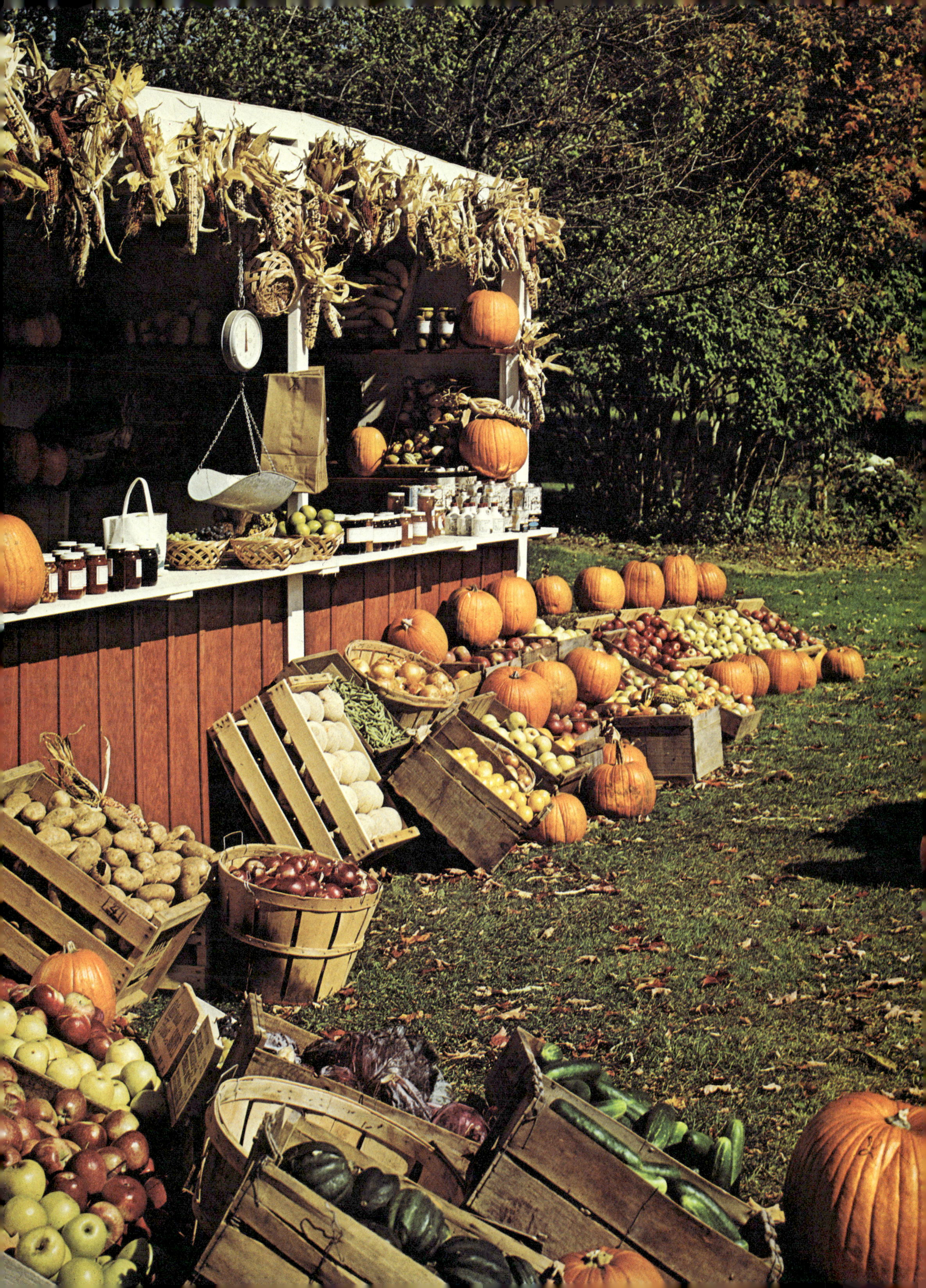

A Summer Past

How the jars and lids were polished up
   And arranged in a sudsy sink
Where they'd bounce around with glassy sound
   And would make their sudden clink,

And the kettles rolled and bubbled
   Cheeseclothed spices through the air,
With the cores and shreds of green and red
   Spread on papers everywhere.

Little lips would lick the labels,
   Little eyes would study so
All the crisp green spears, the citron jams
   And the relish in a row.

And when, on a winter suppertime,
   We would climb down a wooden stair,
We would find, all glassed, a summer past
   And bring it up to share.

Ellen Chambers

Canning Time

It's canning time and my kitchen is sweet
With the fragrance of cinnamon, mace and clove
As sweet, spiced syrup furiously boils
In a granite kettle on top the stove.

And the pears beneath the russet foam
Are clear as honey within the comb.
Packed in jars, on racks to cool,
Are the amber of peach and apricot's gold,

And wine-red plums, all ready to eat
When winter days are short and cold.
Tomorrow they will be stored away...
But my kitchen is fragrant with spices today.

Luella Bender Carr

The Horn of Plenty

O dear God, I give Thee thanks
for the horn of plenty filled with fruits
that flourish in every land upon this earth;
a painter's palette in the red of apple,
purple grape and green of melon;
I give Thee thanks for all the food we eat,
the pod, the stalk, the root and seed.

O dear God, I give Thee thanks
for the horn of plenty, filled and running over
with all the things that make life good...
the fruit of the loom, the carving of the sculptor,
the words of the poet and the artist's canvas
interspersed with the plate, the spoon,
the bed, the board, the roof over all.
I give Thee thanks for all we use each day.

O dear God, I give Thee thanks
for the horn of plenty, invisible but real,
filled with the great abundance of the Spirit,
filled with joy and beauty, wisdom and peace,
filled with creativity, filled with love.
Oh, I give Thee thanks for these intangibles
and for all my brothers on this earth
with whom I share this heritage of life.

Elizabeth Searle Lamb

Copyrighted. Used by
permission of DAILY WORD.

Afterglow

Though summer's vanished,
   all her colors hiding,
Gone the flowers and the
   bluebird's wing,
Still abundant beauty
   is abiding
In brilliant jewels fit
   for a king.
Ruddy apples like red
   rubies blaze;
Fruits are blushing like
   the afterglow
Of sunbeams captured from
   bright summer days;
The horn of plenty's
   lavish overflow
Is like a cheerful light
   against the cold;
And jugs hold amber
   by the cider mill.
The pumpkins stand in
   pyramids of gold
While the tattered scarecrows
   wave from the windy hill.

Ruth B. Field

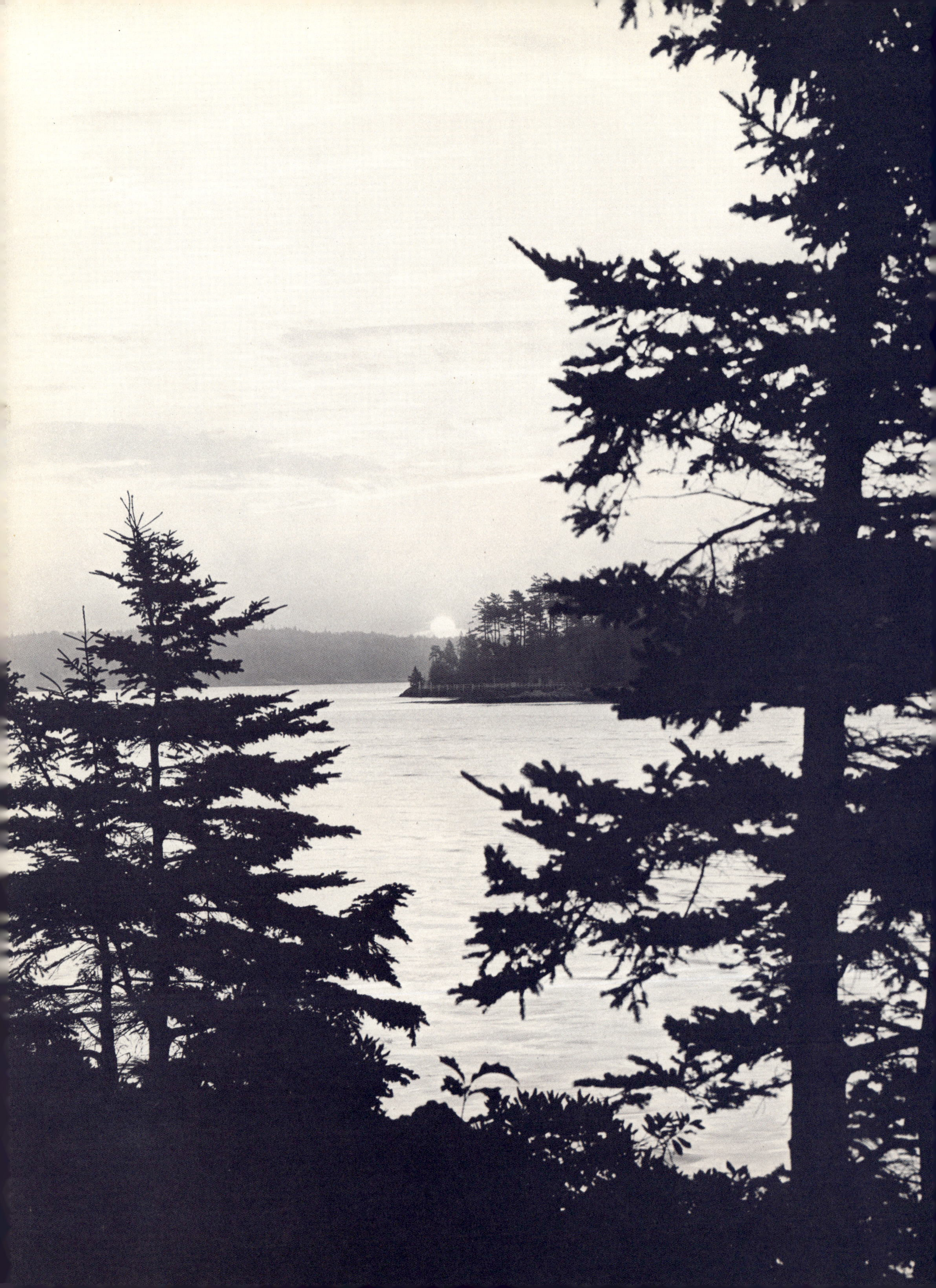

An Autumn at Stillwald

There is a chill in the air this autumn evening at Stillwald, my home on the banks of the Plover River. As shadows begin to lengthen and the sun slowly slips behind the woods, the burnished reds and gold of the twin maples by the old log barn take on more somber hues.

With each brisk breeze, leaves lose their hold on the browned, weathered branches and zigzag gaily to the lawn below. There they skip lightly, swinging and swirling like fairy sprites dancing to the music of the wind. Suddenly they stop as though out of breath, but hardly are given time before another breeze lifts them high in the air. Dipping and soaring on invisible wings, they are carried to the woods beyond, where they join other dried and curling leaves of another autumn night.

A late robin on the lawn cocks his head to listen for an unwary angleworm, one last morsel of food before seeking shelter in the pines for the night. Not long and he will be leaving for a warmer clime where the ground doesn't freeze in the winter.

My thoughts wander and I think of the birds that stay with us the year around. There is the friendly chickadee, the white and rose-breasted nuthatches, the hairy and downy woodpeckers, the saucy blue jays and an occasional slate-colored junco and tree sparrow. Perhaps I will be especially lucky this winter and a cardinal, or red-bird as he is sometimes called, will come for the sunflower seeds I provide. I must get the feeding stations ready to welcome the winter birds.

I am a bit sad in the fall of the year as I contemplate the long period of nature's apparent dormancy. Like humans, she seems to require a time for restoring energy. With sureness born from observing other seasons, I know that where each burnished leaf has lost its hold on the weathered brown branches of this autumn evening, another spring will see a new bud burst forth. Nature in all her springtime splendor will blossom again in a fresh gown of green.

Quietly I watch the curtain of night draw down over Stillwald, my peaceful home among the pines.

Mildred Lonsdorf

November Rain

*I love a soft November rain,
The melody of its refrain
As it falls gently on the ground
Cleansing coverlets of brown,
Foretelling harvest almost past,
Thanksgiving time to come at last
When friends and loved ones gather in
With gratitude for gifts from Him,
The Giver of all perfect gifts,
Who many a heavy burden lifts!*

Agnes Finch Whitacre

Smell of Woodsmoke

Woodsmoke has the nicest smell
And lots of stories it can tell
Of balmy days and crisp, cool nights
And harvest moons with amber lights.

As lazy smoke drifts toward the sky
I see a family sitting by.
Sometimes there's talk, sometimes they dream
And watch the wood fire embers gleam.

Sometimes a picture can be seen
Against the wood fire's lacy screen.
It tells of lovers holding hands
And dreaming dreams and making plans.

Woodsmoke curls and floats away
Like pipe dreams for another day.
I think it has the nicest smell
And lots of stories it can tell.

Laurie E. Dawson

AUTUMN'S SPELL

The fields of wheat are seas of gold
   Along the open country road.
The orchard's wealth clings to the vine,
   Clustered fruit for sweet, red wine.

The cornstalks' silken, tasseled heads
   Stand tall above the melon beds;
The golden pumpkin waits its fate
   To be a jack-o'-lantern's face,

While in the cornfield at his post,
   Reluctant scarecrow's playing host
To crows who taunt his haystack head
   And raid, like beggars, the harvest bed.

The harvesttime is a holiday
   Of brilliant colors, costumes gay,
So Autumn, weave your magic spell
   Ere winter's white shrouds hill and dell.

Edith Elaine Williamson

*Photograph opposite
Photo Media*

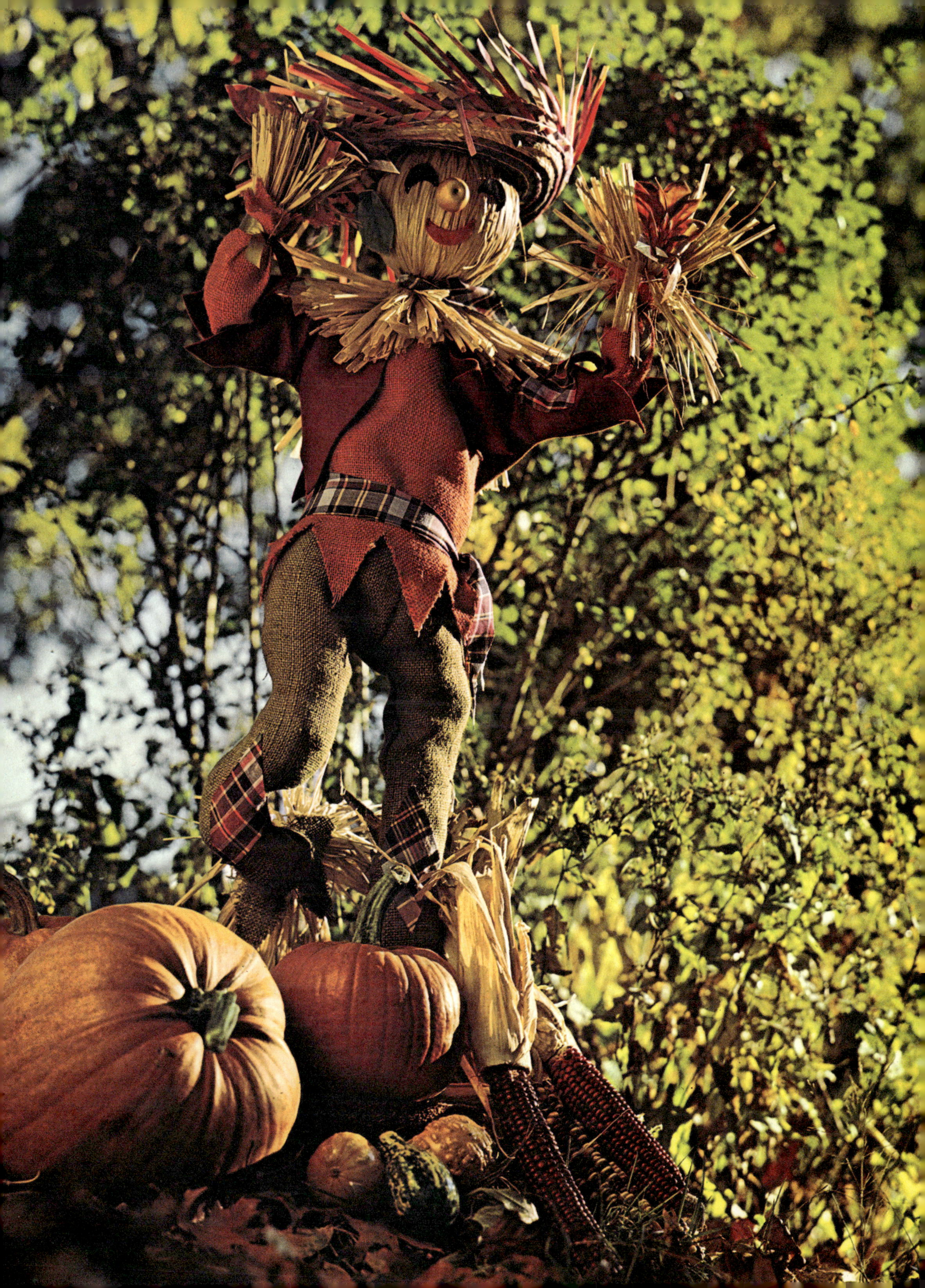

Bobbing for Apples

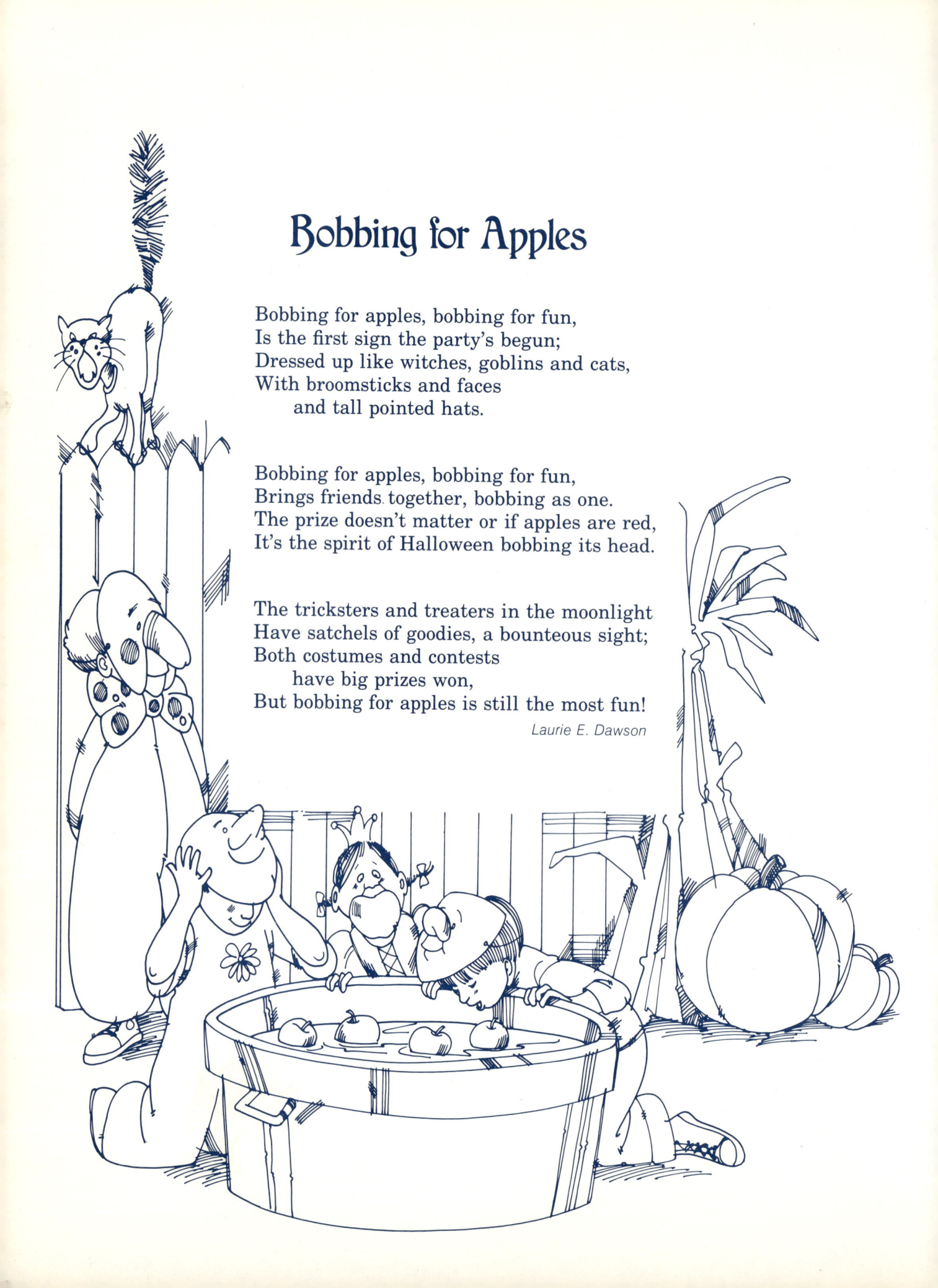

Bobbing for apples, bobbing for fun,
Is the first sign the party's begun;
Dressed up like witches, goblins and cats,
With broomsticks and faces
    and tall pointed hats.

Bobbing for apples, bobbing for fun,
Brings friends together, bobbing as one.
The prize doesn't matter or if apples are red,
It's the spirit of Halloween bobbing its head.

The tricksters and treaters in the moonlight
Have satchels of goodies, a bounteous sight;
Both costumes and contests
    have big prizes won,
But bobbing for apples is still the most fun!

Laurie E. Dawson

Halloween Party Time

A Halloween party—
Hip-hip-hooray!
We've longed and we've waited
For this happy day.

There'll be lots of games,
Pinning on donkey's tail
And dripping wet faces
Bobbing apples from a pail,

A ghost walk for certain
To frighten and scare,
With witches and goblins
Hid round everywhere.

Have you tried eating apples
From a long piece of string?
The onlookers' laughter
Will make the roof ring.

After the games
Are all over once more,
Hot chocolate and doughnuts
To eat by the score!

Ruth H. Underhill

Halloween Visitors

A mouse is standing at my door,
Surely not much over four,
And a lady of two or so, I'd guess,
With ridiculous hat and scary dress.
They both are hoping they will see

Photo Media

Me scared of them as scared can be!
My eyes get round, I shake, in fact
I put on such a convincing act
That two little voices, happy and sweet,
Bravely quiver, "Twick or tweet!"

George L. Ehrman

Fred Sieb

Ichabod Crane's Ride

from "The Legend of Sleepy Hollow"

Washington Irving
(1783-1859)

The "Legend of Sleepy Hollow," you will remember, concerns a quiet 18th century Dutch settlement in the legend-filled valley of the Hudson River, and its homely school teacher, Ichabod Crane.

Both Ichabod and the roguish young Brom Van Brunt sought the hand of Katrina Van Tassel. On the night of the fateful ride, both of Katrina's rivals attended her quilting party. Ichabod lagged behind the departing guests in order to speak to her alone. But Katrina rejected him. And then . . .

The revel gradually broke up. The old farmers gathered together their families in their wagons, and were heard for some time rattling along the hollow roads, and over the distant hills. Some of the damsels mounted on pillions behind their favorite swains, and their lighthearted laughter, mingling with the clatter of hoofs, echoed along the silent woodlands, sounding fainter and fainter until they gradually died away. The late scene of noise and frolic was all silent and deserted.

Ichabod stole forth with the air of one who had been sacking a henroost rather than a fair lady's heart. Without looking to the right or left to notice the scene of rural wealth on which he had so often gloated, he went straight to the stable, and with several hearty cuffs and kicks roused his steed most uncourteously from the comfortable quarters in which he was soundly sleeping.

It was the very witching time of night when Ichabod, heavyhearted and crestfallen, pursued his travel homeward along the sides of the lofty hills which rise above Tarry Town. The hour was as dismal as himself. Far below him the Tappan Zee spread, with here and there the tall mast of a sloop riding quietly at anchor.

In the dead hush of midnight, he could even hear the barking of a watchdog from the opposite shore of the Hudson; but it was so vague and faint as only to give an idea of his distance from this faithful companion of man.

Now and then, too, the long-drawn crowing of a cock accidentally awakened would sound far, far off, from some farmhouse away among the hills. No signs of life occurred near him except occasionally the melancholy chirp of a cricket or perhaps the guttural twang of a bullfrog from a neighboring marsh.

Ichabod could now faintly discern the outline of the church far ahead. It stood on a knoll surrounded by lofty elms. The sequestered situation of this church seems always to have made it a favorite haunt of troubled spirits. A gentle slope descends from it to a silver sheet of water bordered by high trees.

The night grew darker and darker. The stars seemed to sink deeper in the sky, and driving clouds occasionally hid them from his sight. He had never felt so lonely and dismal. In the center of the road stood an enormous tulip tree which towered like a giant above all the other trees of the neighborhood and formed a kind of landmark. It was connected with the tragic story of the unfortunate Andre, who had been taken prisoner hard by. It was universally known by the name of Major Andre's tree. The common people regarded it with a mixture of respect and superstition.

As Ichabod approached this fearful tree, he began to whistle. He thought his whistle was answered. It was but a blast sweeping sharply through the dry branches. As he approached a little nearer, he thought he saw something white hanging in the midst of the tree. He paused and ceased whistling. But on looking more narrowly, he perceived that it was a place where the tree had been scathed by lightning, and the white wood laid bare. Suddenly he hears a groan. His teeth chattered and his knees smote against the saddle. It was but the rubbing of one huge bough upon another as they were swayed by the breeze. He passed the tree in safety, but new perils lay before him.

About two hundred yards from the tree a small brook crossed the road, and ran into a marshy and thickly-wooded glen known by the name of Wiley's swamp. A few rough logs laid side by side served as a bridge over this stream. To pass this bridge was the severest trial. It was at this identical spot that the unfortunate Andre was captured, and this had ever since been considered a haunted stream. Fearful are the feelings of the schoolboy who has to pass it alone after dark.

As he approached the stream his heart began to thump. However, he summoned up all his resolutions, gave his horse half a score of kicks in the ribs and attempted to dash briskly across the bridge. But instead of starting forward, the perverse old animal made a lateral movement and ran broadside against the fence. Ichabod, whose fears increased with the delay, jerked the reins on the other side and kicked lustily with the contrary foot. It was all in vain. His steed started, it is true, but it was only to plunge to the opposite side of the road into a thicket of brambles and alder bushes.

The schoolmaster now bestowed both whip and heel upon the starveling ribs of old Gunpowder, who dashed forward, snuffing and snorting, but came to a stand just by the bridge with a suddenness which nearly sent his rider sprawling over his head. Just at this moment a plashy step by the side of the bridge caught the sensitive ear of Ichabod. In the dark shadow of the grove, on the margin of the brook, he beheld something huge, misshapen, black and towering. It stirred not, but seemed gathered up in the gloom, like some gigantic monster ready to spring upon the traveler.

The hair of the affrighted pedagogue rose upon his head with terror. What was to be done? To turn and fly was now too late. Summoning up, therefore, a show of courage, he demanded in stammering accents, "Who are you?" He received no reply. He repeated his demand in a still more agitated voice. Still there was no answer. Once more he cudgeled the sides of the inflexible Gunpowder, and shutting his eyes, broke forth with involuntary fervor into a psalm tune. Just then the shadowy object of alarm put itself in motion and with a scramble and a bound, stood as once in the middle of the road.

Though the night was dark and dismal, yet the form of the unknown might now in some degree be ascertained. He appeared to be a horseman of large dimensions, and mounted on a black horse of powerful frame. He made no offer of molestation or sociability, but kept aloof on one side of the road, jogging along beside old Gunpowder.

Ichabod, who had no relish for this strange midnight companion, now quickened his steed in hopes of leaving him behind. The stranger quickened his horse to an equal pace. Ichabod pulled up, and fell into a walk, thinking to lag behind. The other did the same. His heart began to sink within him. He endeavored to resume his psalm tune, but his parched tongue clove to the roof of his mouth and he could not utter a stave.

There was something in the moody and dogged silence of this pertinacious companion that was mysterious and appalling. It was soon fearfully accounted for. On mounting a rising ground, which brought the figure of his fellow-traveler in relief against the sky, gigantic in height and muffled in a cloak, Ichabod was horror-struck on perceiving that he was headless!

But his horror was still more increased on observing that the head, which should have rested on his shoulders, was carried before him on the pommel of his saddle! His terror rose to desperation. He rained a shower of kicks and blows upon Gunpowder, hoping by a sudden movement to give his companion the slip. But the specter started full jump with him.

Away then they dashed, through thick and thin, stones flying and sparks flashing at every bound. Ichabod's flimsy garments fluttered in the air as he stretched his long lank body away over his horse's head in the eagerness of his flight.

An opening in the trees now cheered him with the hope that the church bridge was near at hand. The wavering reflection of a silver star in the bosom of the brook told him that he was not mistaken. "If I can but reach that bridge," thought Ichabod, "I am safe."

Just then he heard the black steed panting and blowing close behind him; he even fancied that he felt its hot breath. Another convulsive kick in the ribs, and old Gunpowder sprang upon the bridge. He thundered over the resounding planks; he gained the opposite side. And now Ichabod cast a look behind to see if his pursuer would vanish, according to rule, in a flash of fire and brimstone.

Just then he saw the goblin rising in his stirrups, and in the very act of hurling his head at him! Ichabod endeavored to dodge the horrible missile, but too late. It encountered his cranium with a tremendous crash. He was tumbled headlong into the dust. Gunpowder, the black steed and its goblin rider passed by like a whirlwind.

The next morning the old horse was found without his saddle and with the bridle under his feet, soberly cropping the grass at this master's gate. While beyond the bridge, on the bank of a broad part of the brook where the water ran deep and black, was found the hat of the unfortunate Ichabod. And close beside it lay a shattered pumpkin!

Years later, an old farmer returned from a visit to New York with the news that Ichabod Crane was still alive and prosperous; that he had left the neighborhood in fear of the ghost and embarrassment at having been dismissed by Katrina. Strangely enough, it was observed that Brom Van Brunt, who had won the hand of Katrina, smiled smugly whenever the story was related and always burst into a hearty laugh at the mention of the pumpkin.

LEGEND

A long time ago an American Indian had the idea to invent a lure, an invitation for all wild waterfowl to foregather at hunter's ambush. It was fashioned in the likeness of duck; an artificial canvasback, made of reeds and feathers and colored by native paints. The man cut and tried—and tried again. He made one. He made two. Finally there were more, and when tethered on the water they floated for all the world like a group of wild ducks feeding.

North America was a wilderness then—a land of forests and streams. Over trackless plains, buffalo grass stood high and virgin. In silent mountains lay gold unsought. There were no white men. The vast continent was untilled, unfenced and uninhabited save for roving bands of Indians. And all life was wild.

Over this land of solitude, so long ago, lay the hush of autumn. Day was breaking. In the thatch a northerly wind played. Patches of shell ice glinted in the marsh. Silence was broken only by lapping water and whistle of wings on errands of migration.

The wildfowl of North America were moving southward. Wisps of snipe had come and gone again. Wild geese passed leisurely in the sky. Over the estuary, waterfowl hovered as smoke clung to the sea.

Offshore a few yards, a group of reeded canvasbacks rode crazily at anchor. Mooring lines of twisted grass pitched downward through waving tendrils to stone anchors on wild celery bottom. Behind a flimsy screen of dried grass the red-skinned inventor shivered in the cold. The idea was launched—to live or die.

Joel Barber

Massasoit

Massasoit was the sachem, or great chief, of the Wampanoag Indians, the tribe that lived in what is now southern Massachusetts. He was born in about 1580 and was named Wasamegin, or Yellow Feather. By the time the Pilgrims came to Plymouth, he had earned the right to be addressed as Massasoit, which was a title of great honor.

The Wampanoags had been a mighty and populous tribe until a great epidemic, probably smallpox, afflicted them during the three years before the Pilgrims landed. The great tribe was reduced to a population of about three hundred. By 1620 they had begun to repeople the land, but because of the affects of the epidemic and the inclement season of the year, the colonists saw only one Indian during their first three months in North America.

Later, however, the settlers became acquainted with the Native Americans of the area. One of the most helpful was Tisquantum, whom they called Squanto. He spoke some English and taught the colonists to catch red herrings both to eat and to fertilize their crops. By planting one fish in each hill of corn, the Pilgrims learned to get fair crops from even the sandiest soil.

It was Samoset, however, a local Indian leader, who introduced the colonists to Massasoit and brought the chief to the first Thanksgiving. Massasoit and the colonial governor signed the first diplomatic treaty in North America, an agreement of peace and mutual protection. The treaty remained inviolate throughout the sachem's lifetime.

Massasoit proved to be as kind to individuals in need of help as he was to the colonists as a group. It is reported that when Roger Williams was exiled from the Plymouth colony for espousing unorthodox religious beliefs, Massasoit cared for him for six weeks. The chief stayed in Rhode Island, Williams' colony, until he died in about 1660.

Although he did not spend the last years of his life in the Plymouth colony, Massasoit was remembered. His statue was later erected on a hill overlooking Plymouth Rock. It still stands there to remind the people of Plymouth of the noble chief who helped their ancestors learn to survive in a strange land.

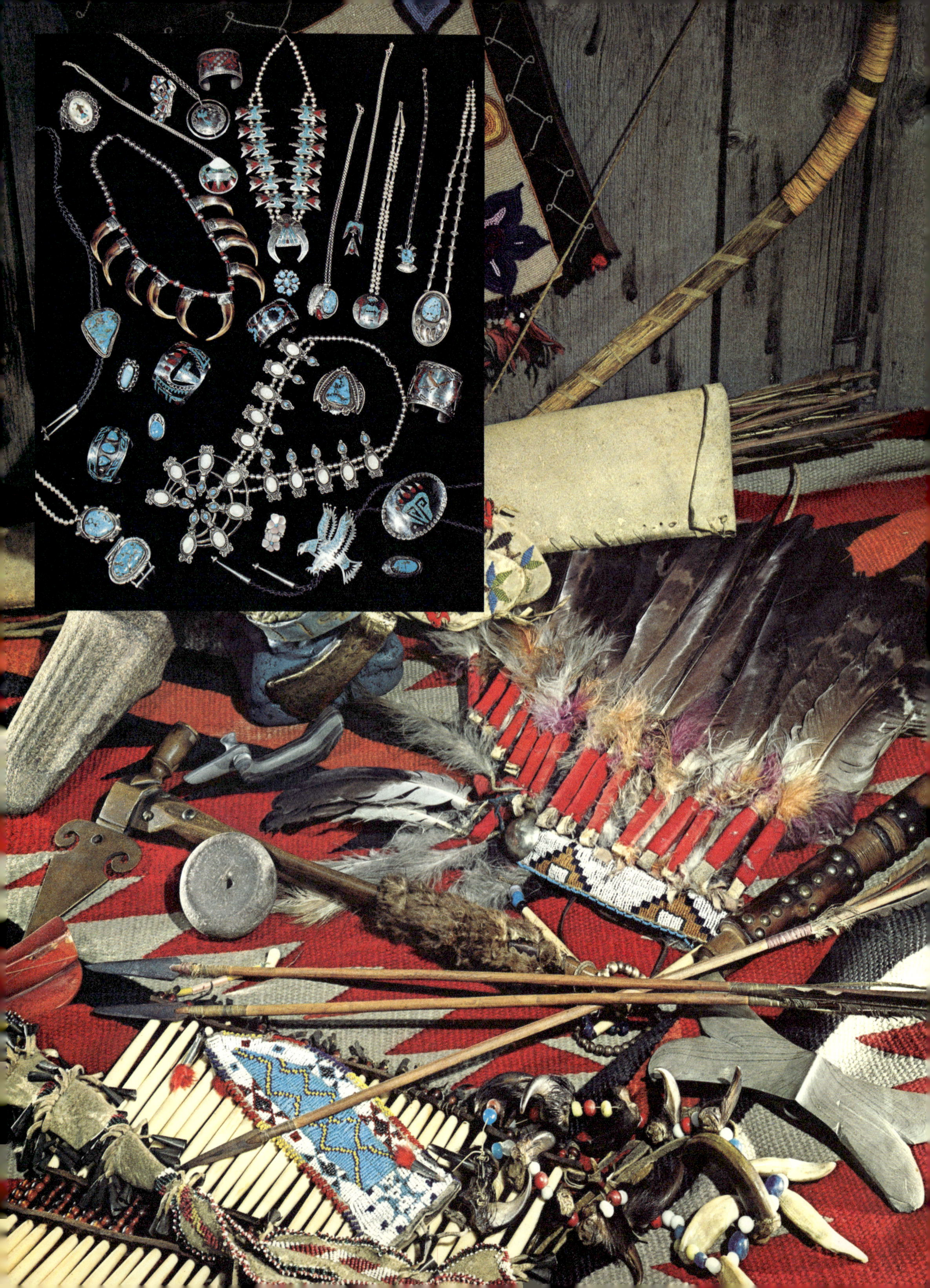

An Indian's Prayer

Oh, great Spirit, whose voice I hear in the winds
And whose breath gives life to everyone,
Hear me.
I come to you as one of your children.
I am weak...I am small...I need your wisdom
  and your strength.
Let me walk in beauty, and make my eyes ever
  behold the red and purple sunsets.
Make my hands respect the things you have made
  and make my ears sharp so I may hear your voice.
Make me wise, so that I may understand what you
  have taught my people and
The lessons you have hidden in each leaf
  and each rock.
I ask for wisdom and strength,
Not to be superior to my brothers, but to be able
  to fight my greatest enemy, myself.
Make me ever ready to come before you with
  clean hands and straight eye,
So as life fades away as a fading sunset,
My spirit may come to you without shame.

Our Indian Heritage

Little do we realize the debt we owe to the American Indian, the first Americans. All over this Western World are to be noted their footsteps. They had an honor and integrity of their own. Unless betrayed, their word could be depended upon.

The early settlers who came from across the seas, many in search of freedom, found a race of human beings who had known freedom for hundreds of years. Unemotional, they had a mind and a culture and a love of nature that few of us today have learned to match. These Indians of America were a quiet-spoken race, physically superb, with an inner depth of soul. Conquered in battle, they were never conquered spiritually. These Indians looked to the Supreme Father over all, and so considered the land under their feet as something that belonged to all. Yet they were driven from place to place, rarely gaining the justice that was their right. They looked upon the earth as their mother and worshipped the sun as the great giver and blessed benefactor. How dependent they were upon all nature!

All over America immortal tribute is paid to our Indian forebears in the names of our towns, cities, rivers, schools and institutions.

Many an Indian has risen to an enduring fame . . . Jim Thorpe, one of the greatest athletes of all time; Will Rogers, the beloved humorist and philosopher, and many others. Charles Curtis, the Kansas United States senator, was well-furnished with Indian blood, and he became vice-president of the United States with Herbert Hoover as president—but once removed from the Presidency!

George Matthew Adams

Copyrighted. Used by permission of Washington Star Syndicate, Inc.

Genuine Indian artifacts from the collection of Gale V. Highsmith. Photograph opposite/Ralph Luedtke

Inset-turquoise jewelry courtesy of Susan L. Fink, Milwaukee, Wis. Photograph–Gerald Koser

"In the Name of God, Amen!"

Lucille Crumley

"In the name of God, amen!"

So opens the Mayflower Compact. This pact was a rule of law for the small settlement of Plymouth, to which all must subscribe before leaving the ship to enter the new land. This document is a masterpiece, which in one sentence provided a workable code under which the people might live in peace and order.

Here it is: "We do, by these presents, solemnly and mutually, in the presence of God and one of another, covenant and combine ourselves together into a civil body politic, for our better ordering and preservation and furtherance of the ends aforesaid; and by virtue hereof enact, constitute and frame such just and equal laws, ordinances, acts, constitutions and offices, from time to time, as shall be thought most meet and convenient for the general good of the colony; unto which we promise all due submission and obedience."

This rule of law and order in all things was the very premise upon which the United States was founded. It was begun in the cabin of the Mayflower with the signing of the above compact. It established the world's first government for and by the people. Although they could not have known what they were starting, the Pilgrims, with one stroke of the pen, created the freedoms, the justice, and the opportunities which have made America unique among the nations of the world.

The Pilgrims left England to escape the yoke of religious persecution, to find a place in a wilderness where they might walk in all His ways, whatever the cost. And in all simplicity and humility, this they did. The Pilgrims brought God to these shores as a partner, comforter, and friend. They brought the Holy Bible as their guide. America was born a Christian nation, thanks to them. They loved God and they loved order. We fell heir to their priceless legacy by their faith and their blood, which they gave that we might be free.

Our American holiday of Thanksgiving is traced to this Plymouth colony, but the idea is much older. The origin of the custom of setting aside a time of thanksgiving to God is lost in the mists of time. There are repeated references to expressions of thanksgiving in the Old Testament. Noah, delivered from the flood, erected an altar to the Lord in thanksgiving. One can uncover in history many a poignant tableau of thanksgiving. In Revelation we can journey to the island of Patmos and join a prisoner, named John, to behold a future thanksgiving scene that spans the dimensions of time and space, to generate hope and new life in the weariest of human breasts.

We find in Revelation 7:11-12, "And all the angels stood round about the throne . . . and fell before the throne on their faces, and worshipped God, saying, Amen: Blessing, and glory, and wisdom, and thanksgiving, and honour, and power, and might, be unto our God for ever and ever. Amen."

Only the blessed of God know what Thanksgiving Day is really all about. Only the country that was founded, under God, is the greatest blest in 1975. We, the people of today, must preserve this heritage for our children and our children's children, in the name of God, amen!

SIGNING THE MAYFLOWER COMPACT
1620

by J. G. L. Ferris (American, 1863-1930)

Three Lions, Inc.

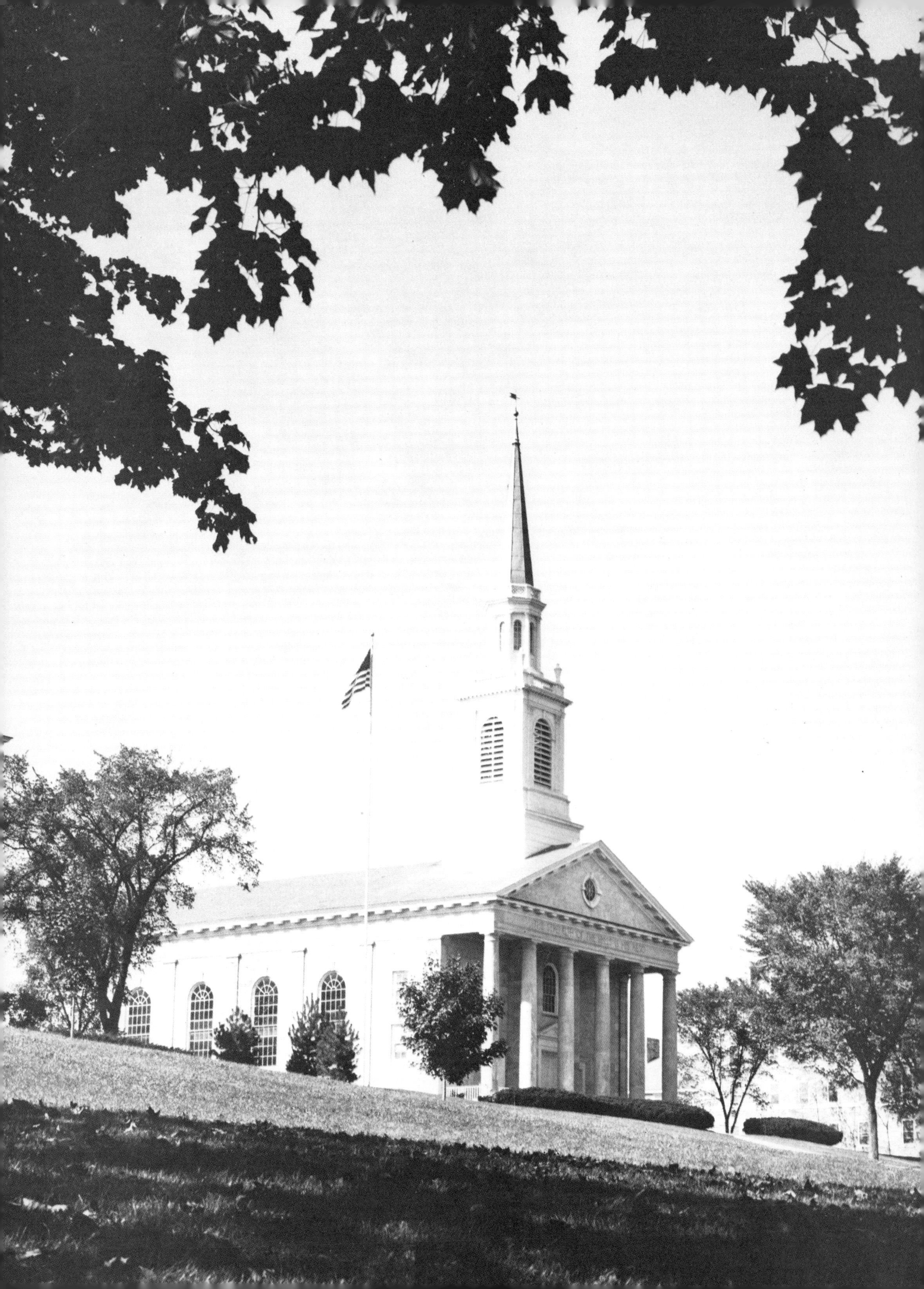

Late Sunshine Lingers on the Hill

Late sunshine lingers on the hill
Across a trail the Indians trod
And seeks a spire where men still
In truth and spirit worship God.

And Plymouth Rock is a milestone passed,
And Valley Forge is a shrine,
And wagon wheels of the pioneers
Have tamed the frontier line.
And the timeless shadow of Lincoln falls
Over a land that's free,
And a nation, tried and tested, lives
"Conceived in liberty."

The flag we love now flies above . . .
We thank Thee, Lord, and pray
Our fathers' faith may keep us strong.
God bless Thanksgiving Day!

E. T. Homme

Thanksgiving-Then and Now

They offered thanks—those Pilgrims strong!
The winter had been cruel and long
But then came spring and summertime
And autumn brought a harvest fine.
And so they knelt, heart-deep in praise
In gratitude for better days.

We offer thanks—we space-age sons—
For blessings shared by everyone,
For freedoms which we still enjoy,
For faith no power can destroy.
Today, we kneel in praise to Thee
For keeping our great nation free!

Nathanael Olson

A Time for All Things

Autumn is the season to harvest
  and be proud.
Autumn is the reason the fertile earth
  was plowed.
God made a time for planting and time
  in which to reap,
So man might learn through labor
  that giving is to keep.

He gave us time to study and time
  to understand,
And time to ease the pain we see
  and lend a helping hand.
We have the time for kindness
  and time to plant a smile,
And there is always time enough
  to walk the second mile.

God made a world of beauty and set it
  in our hand;
He bade us work to tend it as we would
  till the land.
Have we made earnest effort? Do we our
  duties see?
And in the proper season what will our
  harvest be?

Eloise Chisolm

The beautifully colored Currier & Ives clock by Seth Thomas, size 11½" square, shown on the page opposite, is complete with rich pine frame, porcelain dial facing, battery power operated. May be purchased for only $34.95 postpaid. Available through the Special Selections Section on the enclosed order blank.

*Photograph opposite
Gerald Koser*

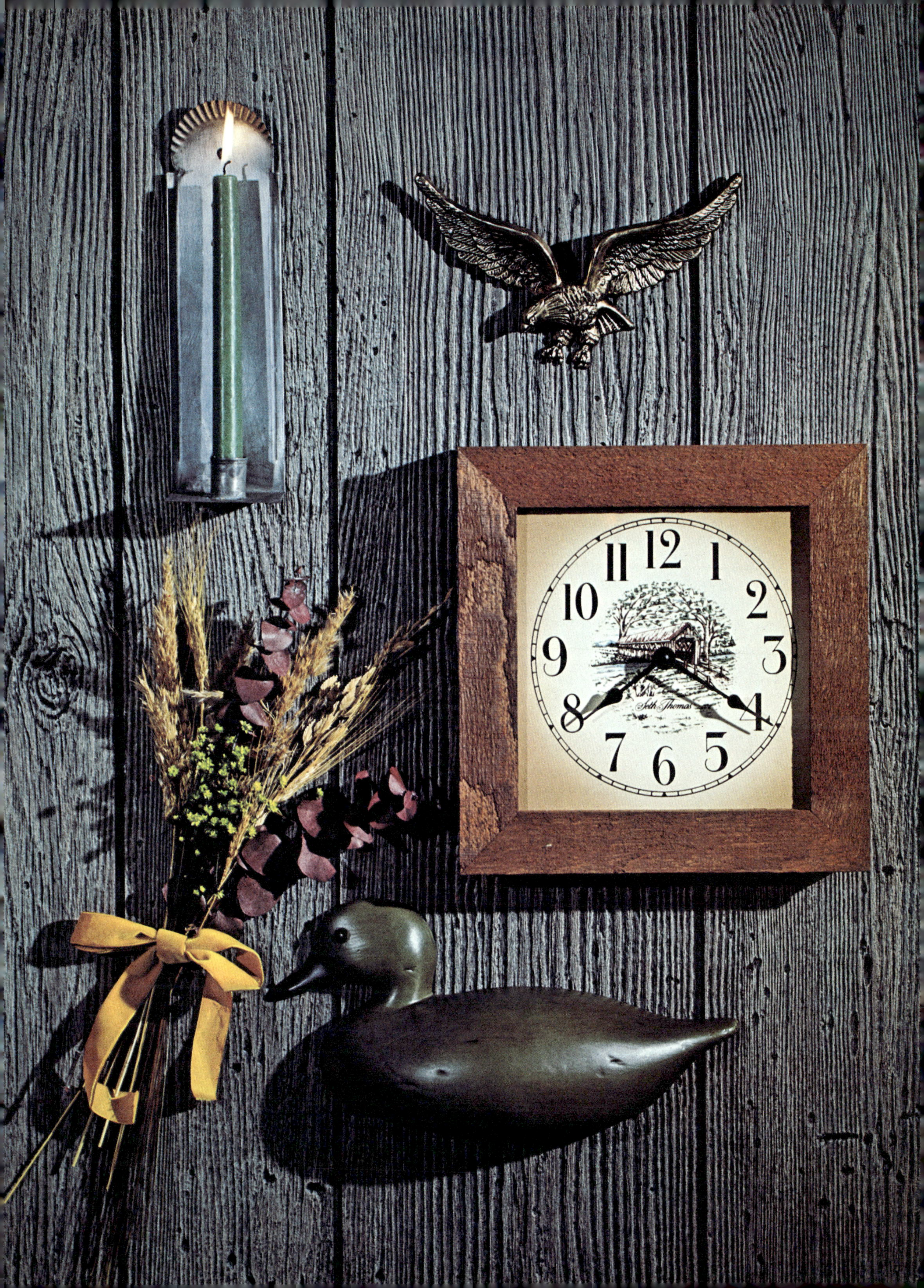

Seth Thomas

Scoot to the Butcher's

Among my thoughtful reflections at Thanksgiving time I find myself often retreating to my boyhood. My thoughts take me back to a rickety little white frame house in a small mining town, the crispness of fall in the air, spicy kitchen smells, and at the table's head my father's deep-toned voice rendering thanks for health and daily bread. And it occurred to me that back in those days when times were a little slower and a little less convenient, we seemed to have more time to be concerned for those around us and for those who needed us. I'd like to tell you one of my earliest reckonings of the importance of kindness and how from this experience I began to learn the meaning of the word grateful.

It began one day with a request by my mother to run an errand to the butcher's—a task that I never minded completing—and on this particular day it was to be one of the more memorable.

"Curt!" called Mother. "Come here a minute." (I could tell she wanted a favor. When I was in trouble, she called me "Curtiss Clinton.")

"I want you to run up to Shank the butcher's and fetch some pork chops for supper. And hurry, because it's almost closing time. Daddy will be home from the mines soon and I want to have his meal ready."

At my urgent plea, she reluctantly agreed to let me ride my scooter to the butcher's. Grandpa had just made it for me in his blacksmith shop and the "new" hadn't worn off yet.

He'd removed the clamps and back brace from my old roller skates. Then he'd fastened the wheels to a 2 by 4 about four feet long. The front end of the homemade scooter was another piece of lumber bolted and braced at right angles to the "running board." He'd trimmed an old hoe handle to make the "steering wheel." The entire vehicle had been painted royal blue. I was tickled to death with that machine.

I scooted lickety-split to Mr. Shank's with Mother's note in my hand. I hitched "Blue Racer" (named after the infamous kind of snakes rumored to hang out in my neighborhood) to the post outside and handed him the order.

"Dear Mr. Shank: Please send me four pork chops—two center cut and thick, two end cut and a little thinner. Be sure to trim off the fat before you weigh them. Put this on our bill and we'll pay you at the end of the month. Mrs. Scarborough."

She'd also given me the verbal instructions: "Watch and make sure he doesn't weigh his thumb with the pork chops." Everybody in town kidded Mr. Shank about that, and he laughed with them. "Shank the butcher has sold his hand many a time," folks said. But they were only teasing. There wasn't a more honest fellow in the county.

Shank's Butcher Shop was about three blocks away from my house. It snuggled tightly between Bennett's Saddlery and Walker's Haberdashery in the town's small business district. Running to the butcher's wasn't a chore to me; it was a pleasure.

The glass front of Mr. Shank's shop came right out to the sidewalk. In that window—depending on the season—he hung geese, turkeys, ducks, cured hams. The bell over the door jangled like mad whenever a customer entered. And inside . . . what delicious smells! The thought of the aroma in that place is enough to make my mouth water even today.

The floor of the shop was covered with sawdust which cushioned each step better than the thickest carpet. (Contrary to neighborhood gossip, Mr. Shank did not sneak some of that sawdust into his ground beef. Or, at least, I never got any splinters between my teeth from his hamburger!)

Two fascinating objects seemed to dominate the room. Mr. Shank cut meat on a big round table. It was a cross-section of an oak tree, about five feet in diameter and two feet thick, with three fat wooden pegs for legs. The table reminded me of a giant milking stool.

The other focal point of the butcher shop was a white metal scale suspended from the rafters. That pointer which told how many pounds of meat you'd bought looked like a clock with a missing hour hand. Beneath it, hanging by three chains, was the platter he put the meat on.

Mr. Shank's tools—knives, cleavers, and a bone saw—each had its proper place on nails driven into the back wall. And there was a big door with an unusual steel latch which led into the walk-in refrigerated back room. I never went inside there, but I did occasionally get a glimpse of sides of beef snagged on large fishhooks.

Mr. Shank cut my pork chops exactly as ordered, wrapped the meat in brown paper and tied it with a string. I fastened the package to my handlebar and hopped on "Blue Racer." As I headed for home I noticed Mr. Shank was starting to lock up for the night.

I also noticed something else. A bunch of stray dogs seemed to be interested in my supper. I put my scooter into high gear and headed for the house. But my sudden acceleration must have whetted their appetites, for a glance over my shoulder confirmed my worst fears. They were in hot pursuit.

I pushed the throttle to the floorboard, squeezed a tiny bit more speed out of "Blue Racer," and then . . . doom! The front wheels caught in a crack in the sidewalk, and I took a flying header. I landed on my right knee and the hungry hounds landed on my pork chops.

Mr. Shank came out of his shop just in time to see the hit and run pooches leaving the scene of the accident. He hurried to the spot where I'd sprawled and surveyed the damage. Without a word, he carried me and my scooter back into his shop. He pulled up my torn overall leg and poured iodine into the gash. His medicine hurt my knee some, but my body wasn't injured nearly as badly as my feelings were.

He saw that, too. And he brought four more cut-to-order pork chops out of the back room. Through my tears, I observed that the cost of those replacements did not get recorded on our credit bill. Then he stuck the meat under his arm and pushed me all the way home on my scooter.

Supermarkets and chain grocery stores are convenient, I suppose. You can get your meat precut, preweighed, prepackaged and precooked. Mass production and modern convenience is progress, and I'm not against it.

But what I'm trying to say is this: no supermarket I ever heard of today will bandage up a boy's knee, give him free pork chops and escort him safely home through a pack of ravenous wolves. Now that's what I call *real* personal service!

Because he had the time to extend this goodwill, for which I was most thankful, Mr. Shank will always be a part of my memories at Thanksgiving time.

Curt Scarborough

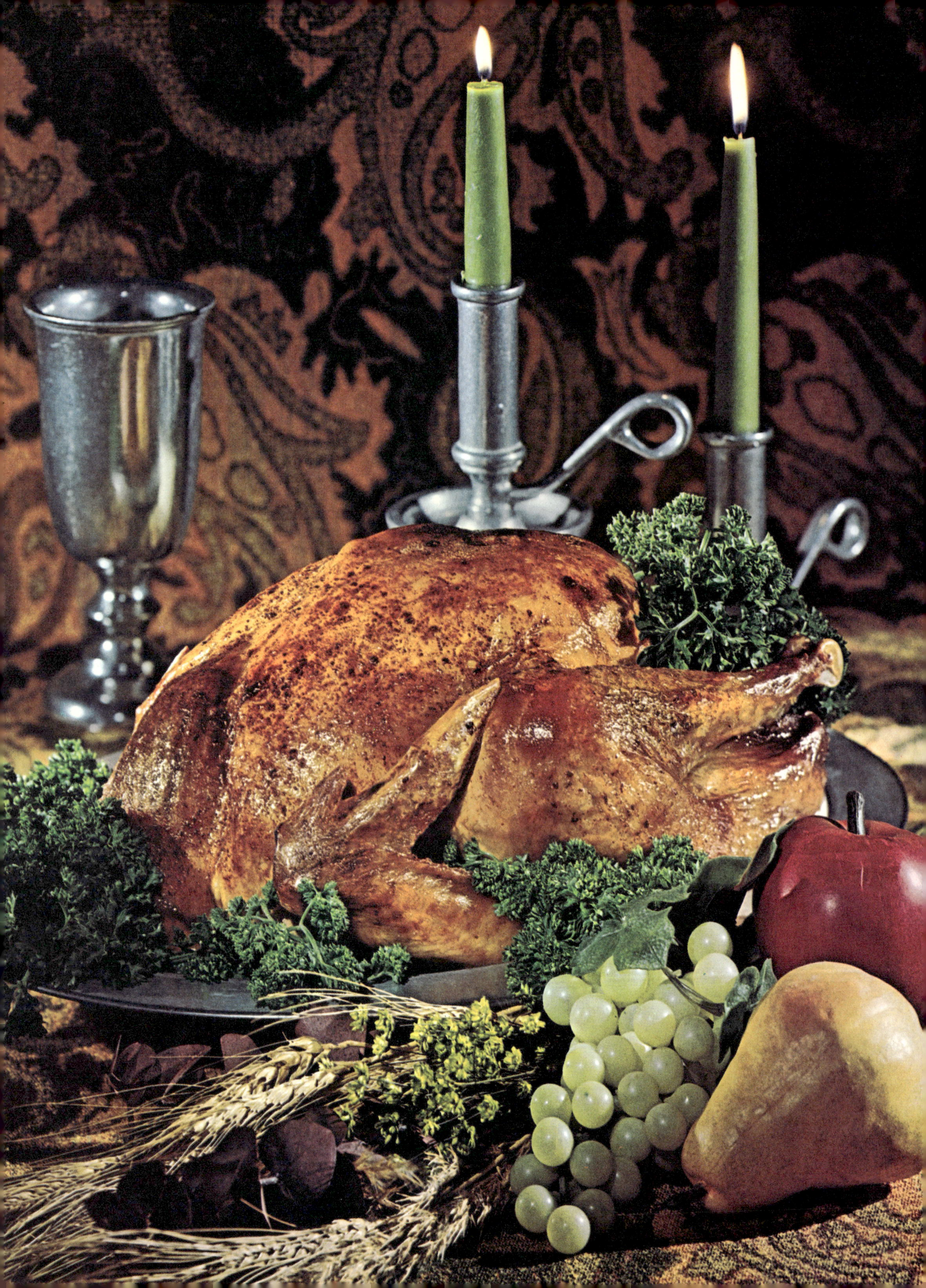

Thanksgiving Prayer

Dear God, as round the table we
Are gathered by Thy grace,
We pause to thank Thee for this food
And for each smiling face.
How wonderful that we can share
These moments once again
With those we love but seldom see—
How long the time has been!
We thank You for Thanksgiving Day,
This special time of year
When we can meet with pleasure all
The ones we hold so dear.
Bless those of us now far away;
Please let their spirits be
Here with us round this table, Lord—
One happy family.
And as we take our places here
And fill our plates with food,
Lord, may our hearts and minds be filled
With special gratitude.

Amen

Phyllis C. Michael

Photograph opposite
Gerald Koser

Thanksgiving at Grandma's House

Across the hills at Grandma's house
The turkey will be baking,
And pumpkin pies and cakes and sweets
Her nimble hands are making.
The oyster dressing's in the stove
And giblet gravy's cooking,
And from the kitchen windowsill
I know old Tabby's looking.

Across the hills at Grandma's house
I see the chestnuts roasting
And all around the open fire
The children's toes are toasting.
The cider mugs are filled with care
And gingerbread is baking,
And Jack Frost at the windowpanes
A new design is making.

Across the hills at Grandma's house
Thanksgiving Day is coming,
And every room is filled with joy
And thankful hearts are humming.
With loved ones on the road for home
A cheerful tune a-singing,
The dinner bell at Grandma's house
With joyful thanks is ringing!

Laurie E. Dawson

Don't Forget the Little Things

Should you start to count your blessings
In the usual, offhand way,
Much like taking inventory
As of this Thanksgiving Day,
You'll no doubt list those outstanding
With a joy that thrills and clings;
But you'll have a happier total
If you'll count the little things!

Don't forget the smiling welcome
Of the one you love so well,
Nor the peaceful evening hour
And the fireside's tranquil spell;
Don't forget the merry prattle
Of that bright-eyed little tad,
Who perhaps loves 'Mummy' mostest,
Yet is crazy 'bout his Dad!

There are many, many blessings,
If we choose to count them all,
And it's only right to list them
With the source from which they fall;
So when taking inventory,
Note the pleasure each one brings,
But be sure to make full entry—
Don't forget the little things!

Adam N. Reiter

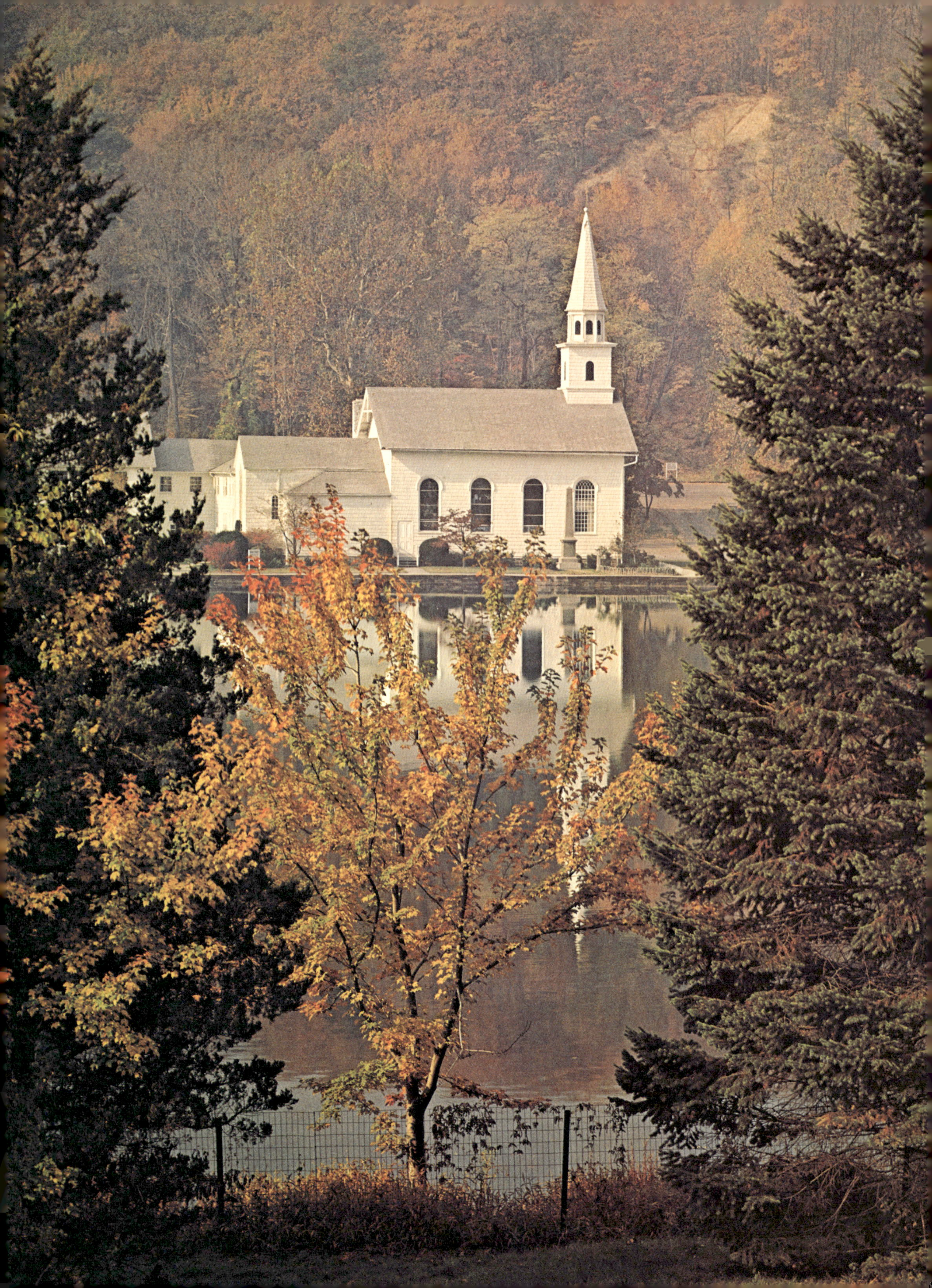

God's Corner

"For the earth shall be filled with the knowledge of the glory of the Lord as the waters cover the sea." That verse was uppermost in my mind as I drove and walked through flaming trails of autumn's most vibrant beauty. The colors are only a matter of memory now. A few leaves drift slowly down, but for the most part the birches and maples stand barren, their branches etched like supplicating arms against a blue sky. And as I scuffle through the yellow and red and gold remnants of nature's most dramatic season, I am filled with thanksgiving at the glory of the Lord as it fills the earth.

As I walk along, I am moved to paraphrase in this fashion: For the earth shall be filled with the knowledge of the presence and power of the Lord. If you are walking with me, you too must feel the impact of this Infinite Invisible that holds a universe in orderly progression. You too must sense the comforting peace that always follows an acknowledgment of God's presence and God's power. It is as though we were literally living and moving and having our being in God. You notice we have no need for conversation. This is a silent time, a time for letting ourselves be filled with thanksgiving that the presence and power of God are governing our every experience.

The giving of thanks expands one's thinking processes. It takes one's mind off the material, the petty, the limiting and opens up a wideness, a depth of thought that leads one into the infinite. Therefore, it is quite natural that another paraphrase should present itself. This concerns itself with a quality inherent in the Infinite Invisible: For the earth shall be filled with the knowledge of the *love* of the Lord. What a picture that evokes—a universe filled to overflowing with a love so warm, so compassionate, so understanding that no one individual, no matter how unhappy or confused or depraved or ill, can be separated from it if he will but open up his consciousness to it. Can you not envisage an entire universe encircled with love? Bound together with love? Then indeed will be fulfilled the promise in Isaiah: "And they shall beat their swords into plowshares, and their spears into pruning hooks: nation shall not lift up sword against nation, neither shall they learn war any more."

Thanksgiving is not an occasion. Thanksgiving is a state of spiritual mindedness. It is a joyous acknowledgment that "... the Lord's hand is not shortened that it cannot save; neither his ear heavy, that it cannot hear." It is a complete acceptance that "It is God that girdeth me with strength, and maketh my way perfect." Thanksgiving is a willingness to accept the omnipresence and omnipotence and love of an Infinite Invisible, and then just "Be still, and know that I am God."

Gertrude M. Puelicher

Photograph opposite
Fred Sieb

Autumn Said "Farewell!"

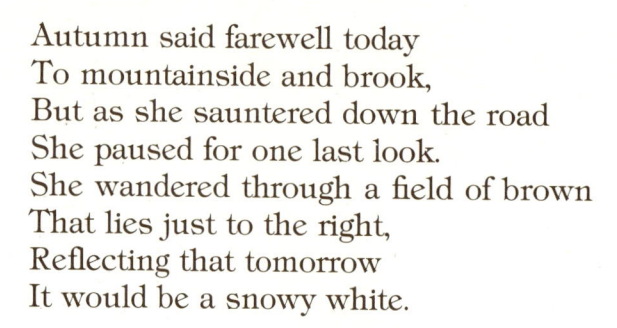

Autumn said farewell today
To mountainside and brook,
But as she sauntered down the road
She paused for one last look.
She wandered through a field of brown
That lies just to the right,
Reflecting that tomorrow
It would be a snowy white.

She stopped beside a cedar tree
With branches thick and green,
Tomorrow it would decorate
A pretty winter scene.
Autumn said farewell today
And raised her russet hand
In fond good-bye to everything
Within the quiet land.

She packed her little treasures
And the rest she stored with care,
So when she comes again next year
She's sure to find them there.
And brushing back a maple leaf
That blew across her face,
She took her colors and her brush
...To paint another place.

Grace E. Easley

ACKNOWLEDGMENTS

Excerpt from WILD FOWL DECOYS by Joel Barber. Dover Publications, Inc., New York, 1954. Reprinted through permission of the publisher. A VAGABOND SONG by Bliss Carman. Reprinted by permission of DODD, MEAD & COMPANY, INC. from BALLADS & LYRICS by Bliss Carman. Copyright 1924 by Dodd, Mead & Company, Inc. CRISP OCTOBER HOURS by Lansing Christman. From "A Hillside Harvest" by Lansing Christman. Copyright 1957 by Lansing Christman and the Taylor Powell Press. ONLY OCTOBER KNOWS by Maude Dickinson. Previously published in The Tacoma News Tribune. TUNNEL OF GOLD by Olive C. Leary. Previously published in AMERICAN BARD, Spring, 1950. THANKSGIVING...THEN AND NOW by Nathanael Olson. Copyright 1974. Nat Olson Publications. GOD'S CORNER by Gertrude M. Puelicher. Previously published in EXCLUSIVELY YOURS. Our sincere thanks to the following authors whose addresses we were unable to locate for material in this book: A. L. Fisher for NOW THE DEER COME BACK; Jennie Pendleton Hall for COVERED BRIDGES; Herbert Walton for SOLILOQUY OF A PUMPKIN by Milly Walton.

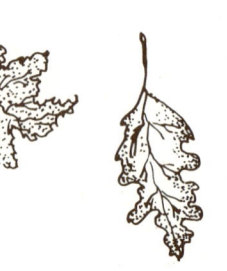

Additional photo credits: Front cover: Colour Library International. Inside front and back covers: Richard W. Brown. Back cover: Arnout Hyde, Jr.

FOR THE ENRICHMENT OF DAILY LIVING . . . READ IDEALS

CHRISTMAS IDEALS . . .

The Spirit Of The Season To Keep And To Share

All the joyous magic, wonder, sacredness, and beauty of the happiest of all seasons will be found among the pages of the sparkling, colorful CHRISTMAS IDEALS 1975.

Share with us the origins of some of the traditional Christmas customs such as the Christmas tree, mistletoe, the Yule log and holly. Young and old alike will truly enjoy a heartwarming short story of the past by Taylor Caldwell, "My Christmas Miracle." Beautiful full color artwork combines with the words of the Gospels as the age-old story of the Nativity unfolds with its inspiring message. Enjoy a feature that tells in word and color photos of Christmases celebrated in America in the 17th, 18th, and 19th centuries. There's a delightful new feature on music boxes and a rich blending of poetry, prose and pictures of all that makes Christmas, that most wonderful time of the year.

You'll love Christmas Ideals 1975 . . . and so will friends and loved ones whom you remember with a delightful gift copy or subscription beginning with this beautiful issue.

See page 6b for subscription information

Single copy price, Only $2.50
Size 8½ x 11 inches — Softcover

DISTINCTIVE CHRISTMAS BOOKS AND GREETING BOOKLETS
For Friends and Loved Ones of All Ages

THE NIGHT BEFORE CHRISTMAS — The anticipation of Santa's arrival has never been so beautifully expressed. This enchanting book contains twenty-four colorful paintings depicting this wonderful old story written by Clement C. Moore. A welcome gift to be read and reread year after year. Softcover — 24 pages

RELIGIOUS CHRISTMAS STORIES F CHILDREN — Liberally sprinkled with color an lustration, this lovely collection of Christmas stories impress children with the spiritual joys and religi meaning of Christmas. Softcover — 32 pages

THE HAPPY CHRISTMAS STORYBOOK — Many hours of childhood pleasure are packed into this new book of Christmas stories. It's filled with old time favorites and selected most popular stories published in previous issues of Ideals. The perfect stocking-stuffer for those special children on your list. — 44 pages

JOLLY OLD SANTA CLAUS — A colorfully il trated visit to Santa's Cookie Kitchen, Toy Shop, fice, and the Christmas Tree Forest. The delightful s of Santa, his Reindeer, and Mrs. Claus preparing their annual Christmas journey. The perfect gift children on your list. Softcover — 40 pages

Children's Books—Only $1.25 each.

SX515 CLOTHESPIN PEOPLE ORNAMENT KIT — To decorate your Christmas tree, or prepare gifts for friends. The kit includes 20 different, enchanting clothespin people ornaments: old-style wood clothespins, non-toxic paints and glue (safe for children), paint brush, sandpaper, all material for trim, gold cord hangers, and simple, illustrated instructions. Only $5.50, plus 50¢ postage per kit. To order, see back of order blank.

LARGER BOOKS SHOWN
ACTUAL SIZE 8½"x11"

CHRISTMAS AROUND THE WORLD — The festivities, the traditions, the pageantries, the special food recipes and popular carols used in the observance of Christmas by the people of Sweden, Germany, Italy, Poland, France, and many others — a total of 16 countries. 24 color pages, with appropriate illustrations, provide a fascinating book for your own enjoyment, and for gift giving. Hardcover — 80 pages — Only $3.50

CHRISTMAS SAMPLER — The Nativity story, the first New England Christmas, old cards and carols with Yuletide customs in many lands and interesting features by Pearl Buck and Lincoln Steffens add a particularly joyful note to this new colorful gift book from Ideals. A wonderful gift to be treasured and enjoyed for many Christmases. Hardcover — 80 pages — Only $3.50

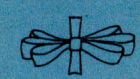

CHRISTMAS GREETINGS — Remember loved ones and friends with this beautiful seasonal greeting booklet, so rich in inspiration, gaity, and every wonderful aspect of the joyous Christmas season.

MISTLETOE AND HOLLY — A light-hearted and contemporary greeting for young and old alike. Poetry, prose and colorful Christmas photos capture the mood of this most festive season.

JOY TO THE WORLD — A delightful songbook for carolers featuring twelve of the all time favorite songs of the season. A practical and useful way of sending holiday cheer to those you love.

ALL GREETINGS — Only 75¢ — 24 pages — 5⅜" x 7¼"
With Mailing Envelopes

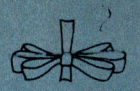

"NEW" FOR CHRISTMAS

THE JOYS OF CHRISTMAS — is . . . remembering, the spirit of giving, the fun of caroling, of baking cookies, trimming the tree, reading by the fire . . . but most of all, Christmas is sharing with family and friends. "The Christmas Story" and short stories by Hamlin Garland and Louise Ingalls Wilder and others help gather the season's joy. Hardcover — 96 pages — Only $4.95

THE IDEALS CHRISTMAS COOKBOOK — Prepare for the Holiday Season with recipes for festive gatherings, and Holiday meals. Written in simple terms are mouth watering recipes for Christmas treats, beverages, meats, and vegetables, with special recipe tips for homemade gifts for friends and family. Add the Ideals touch of beautiful color photographs, sprinkle with a bit of poetry, and blend with over 250 recipes, and you have a delightful book to help you this Holiday Season. Softcover — 64 pages — Only $1.75.

SX514 SANTA'S BOOT — This charming little table decoration for the Holiday Season will surely add a special touch of Christmas spirit wherever it is displayed. It has dozens of decorative uses as a candy dish, pencil holder, or as featured below — a delightful setting for a Christmas planter of holly or poinsettia (up to 4½" in diameter). Completely washable, for years of useful enjoyment. Santa's Boot measures a full 8" x 6½" x 5", and is priced at just $2.99, plus 25¢ postage, each. To order, see back of order blank.

THE IDEALS GIFT SHOPPE SPECIAL SELECTIONS ORDER HERE (See Catalog & Publication)

QUANTITY	CODE NO.	DESCRIPTION	COLOR OR TYPE	AMOUNT	POST. & HAND.	TOTAL & AMOUNT

TOTAL AMT. OF MERCHANDISE _____
WIS. SALES TAX 4% (RESIDENTS) _____
POSTAGE & HANDLING _____
TOTAL AMOUNT OF SALE _____

NOTES BY IDEALS 4 x 5 @ $1.25 SPECIAL CHOOSE ANY 4 BOX SETS AND DEDUCT $ .50

BOX 1 @ 1.25	BOX 15 @ 1.25	BOX 22 @ 1.25	BOX 26 @ 1.25
BOX 2 @ 1.25	BOX 18 @ 1.25	BOX 23 @ 1.25	BOX 27 @ 1.25
BOX 4 @ 1.25	BOX 19 @ 1.25	BOX 24 @ 1.25	BOX 28 @ 1.25
BOX 9 @ 1.25	BOX 20 @ 1.25	BOX 25 @ 1.25	BOX 29 VARIETY
BOX 10 @ 1.25	BOX 21 @ 1.25		PACK @ 1.25

1976 GOURMET CALENDAR BY IDEALS @ $2.50
FRAMES 8½ x 11 FRUITWOOD—CUSTOM MADE—WITH GLASS (SX540) @ $8.50 EA. (Pictured in HARVEST TIME IDEALS)
CURRIER & IVES DECORATOR CLOCK by Seth Thomas (BATTERY RUN) @ $34.95 (Pictured in HARVEST TIME IDEALS)
LOOSE-LEAF RECIPE BOOK—COLORFUL ORGANIZER (5¾ x 6⅜) @ $6.00 (Pictured in IDEALS CHRISTMAS COOK BOOK)

FOLD HERE FIRST

Wisconsin Residents Please Note:
You must Add 4% sales tax on all products sent to Wisconsin addresses, except bimonthly IDEALS issues and subscriptions to IDEALS bi-monthly issues.

☐ IF YOU WISH TO RECEIVE OUR IDEALS CATALOG CHECK HERE. ENTER FRIEND'S NAMES UNDER GIFT AREA OR SEPARATE SHEET.

☐ SEND FUND RAISING INFORMATION

☐ SEND BUSINESS GIFT INFORMATION

ideals PUBLISHING CORP.
11315 WATERTOWN PLANK RD.
MILWAUKEE, WISCONSIN 53201

from _____
( ) _____
ZIP CODE

THANK YOU!

FOLD SIDE FLAPS FIRST — THEN FOLD HERE

FOLD SIDE FLAPS FIRST
When properly sealed with the above gummed flap this envelope and its contents will travel safely through the mail.

FOR OFFICE USE ONLY

ENTRD		TYPE	AMT
REMTC		IDEALS	
K	Mo	C	SUBS	
Checked for Accuracy		BINDER	
		PRINTS	
OVER PAY		POSTAGE	
		ALL'D PROD	
		P.A.Y.R.	
		NOTES	
		TAX	

HARVEST TIME IDEALS

FOLD HERE FIRST

IDENTIFY AS A GIFT FROM _____
TO _____
ADDRESS _____
CITY _____ STATE _____ ZIP CODE ( ) _____
MAIL DATE & OCCASION _____

QUANTITY	TITLE	PRICE
	*4 Vol. Subscription (4 issues)	@ $ 6.00
	*1 Yr. Subscription (6 issues)	@ $ 8.50
	*2 Yr. Subscription (12 issues)	@ $16.00
	LIST OTHER GIFT SELECTIONS BELOW	

SEND CATALOG ☐

IDENTIFY AS A GIFT FROM _____
TO _____
ADDRESS _____
CITY _____ STATE _____ ZIP CODE ( ) _____
MAIL DATE & OCCASION _____

QUANTITY	TITLE	PRICE
	*4 Vol. Subscription (4 issues)	@ $ 6.00
	*1 Yr. Subscription (6 issues)	@ $ 8.50
	*2 Yr. Subscription (12 issues)	@ $16.00
	LIST OTHER GIFT SELECTIONS BELOW	

SEND CATALOG ☐

NOTE..... *Your Subscription will begin with HARVEST TIME unless otherwise indicated _____
IF YOU WISH TO ENTER A CHRISTMAS GIFT SUBSCRIPTION BEGINNING WITH CHRISTMAS 1975—PLEASE ☐ ✔